Praise for *Law, Reinvented: Leading AI Transformation in Legal Practice*

'This book is a goldmine of practical guidance, written by a strong triumvirate of well-credentialed experts. It is refreshingly balanced, steering a sensible middle course between the unbridled enthusiasm and the stultifying caution that currently threaten the productive use of AI in law.'

— **Professor Richard Susskind**, author of *Tomorrow's Lawyers* and *The Future of Law*

'A superb exposition of legal's industrial revolution. There will be a before and an after – this book shows a path between the two. An excellent road map to surviving and thriving in the era of Agentic Law. Read now before it is too late.'

— **Paul Lewis OBE**, Firmwide Managing Partner, Linklaters

'*Law, Reinvented* is a sharp, practical guide to the forces reshaping the legal profession, exploring how AI is redefining client value, recruiting, talent development, and service delivery. Written by practitioners at the forefront of this shift, it reflects real-world experience – not theory. It's not about simply adopting new tools; firms that approach AI as an enterprise-wide transformation will be the ones that truly get ahead. Essential reading for those determined not just to adapt, but to lead.'

— **Kay Kim**, Chief Practice Innovation Officer, Paul Hastings

'*Law, Reinvented* is THE indispensable guide to artificial intelligence in the legal profession. It is both up-to-date and authoritative in its coverage of the topic. The three authors – each an experienced leader of innovation at a major law firm – lucidly explain where we are and how we got here, and then offer practical advice on a path forward. Highly recommended.'

— **Jeffrey Rovner**, Knowledge Management Leader & Technologist

'This book meets the moment the legal profession is in. It does not focus on the shiny tech and instead explores the thorny issues we are all grappling with, including strategy, data, people, training, pricing and processes. It is written by people who have been doing the work, not just talking about it. If you are working in innovation or legal ops, you will undoubtedly recognise a lot and walk away with a few uncomfortable but useful questions to help you think a bit harder about what comes next.'

— **Dr Catriona Wolfenden**, Director of Product and Innovation, Partner, Weightmans

'Congratulations are due to the authors on crafting a truly accessible and comprehensive guide to navigating the challenge of embedding AI in your legal practice. Readers at all levels of the industry will benefit from this timely contribution at a critical moment of transition for the practice of law.'

— **Chris Howard**, University Partnerships Director, BARBRI

'A "must buy" for members of AI and innovation committees in law! The targeted chapters tackle all key considerations for implementing AI in legal. This easy read breaks down the otherwise-daunting challenges into logical and practical steps for effective and sustainable change.'

— **Alicia Hardy**, Director of Knowledge and Learning, Carey Olsen

'A thoughtful and grounded take on how AI is intersecting with the real structural pressures in the legal profession. There are many views on the eventual destination out there, but this is a well-judged contribution to an important conversation.'

— **Paul Greenwood**, Chief Technology Officer, Clifford Chance LLP

LAW, REINVENTED

LAW, REINVENTED

Leading AI Transformation in Legal Practice

Adam Curphey
Oz Benamram
Rebecca Pasternak

LONDON PUBLISHING PARTNERSHIP

Published by London Publishing Partnership
www.londonpublishingpartnership.co.uk

ISBN: 978-1-916749-75-7 (pbk)
ISBN: 978-1-916749-76-4 (iPDF)
ISBN: 978-1-916749-77-1 (ePUB)

A catalogue record for this book is
available from the British Library

This book has been composed in
Adobe Garamond Pro

Copy-edited and typeset by
T&T Productions Ltd, London
www.tandtproductions.com

Printed and bound in Great Britain
by Hobbs the Printers Ltd

Contents

Contents

Preface

THE WHY

The legal profession is in the middle of a transformation unlike anything that has come before. Rapid advancements in AI have not simply added new tools to the lawyer's desk, they have begun to reshape how legal work is performed, how it is priced, how teams are structured, and what clients expect from their advisors. For the first time, questions are being asked about each of these issues simultaneously, and the profession does not yet have settled answers to any of them.

This book is a practical guide for legal professionals who are navigating that uncertainty. It is not a technical manual. It is a book about strategy, people, data, and organizational change, written by three practitioners who work in this space every day and who wanted to bring together what they are seeing, learning, and advising on into a single, cumulative source. While this book will be a support for those in leadership roles, or those preparing to step into them, it is also for those seeking to understand the state of AI in the legal profession and the commercial and strategic pressures that those in leadership are dealing with.

The book is structured around the decisions that legal leaders face in roughly the order they tend to arise. It begins with what is changing and why it matters, and then moves through how the technology works, the strategic implications for pricing and business models, how to build the right team, why data is emerging as the real competitive asset, and how to drive training and adoption. From there it covers tool selection; risk and governance; the rise of lawyer-built solutions and shadow AI; how the relationships between firms, clients, and technology vendors are being reconfigured; and, finally, how to keep pace with a market that moves faster than any single organization can track.

Our goal is both to help you prepare for the change that is already underway and to give you a practical framework for building your own strategy, reviewing your current strategy, or understanding the factors that helped to create the strategy your organization is following. Our hope is that this book will serve as a guide to cut through the noise and enable you to move forward with purpose.

THE WHO

Having three authors rather than one was an intentional choice. Each of us brings a different perspective, having worked directly with and consulted for firms on both sides of the Atlantic, across different practice areas and organizational models. Where we agree, the book reflects that consensus. Where we see things differently, we have tried to present the various perspectives honestly. It should also be noted that any views expressed are our own and are not those of our respective organizations.

Although our combined professional experience has been in large law firms, the principles we discuss apply equally to in-house legal teams, smaller firms, and solo practitioners. Readers should approach the text through whichever lens best reflects their own practice.

THE HOW: DRINKING OUR OWN CHAMPAGNE

There is a saying in technology about 'eating your own dog food', meaning that those who champion a technology should use it themselves. We prefer the more refined phrasing, 'drinking your own champagne'. In that spirit, AI was used throughout the writing of this book. Our process began with the creation of a detailed outline, after which the three of us met weekly to discuss each chapter in depth. We used AI to transcribe those conversations, then fed both the transcripts and our outline notes into AI tools to help refine the initial drafts. Each chapter was then further reviewed and amended by hand, and reviewed again by whichever co-authors had not performed the initial edits. AI also helped us identify gaps and inconsistencies across chapters and flag areas where sources were needed. Sam Clark and Richard Baggaley at London Publishing Partnership then applied their expertise in copyediting and production to transform our text into the finished book you now hold.

It was a genuinely exciting process, not least because our writing coincided with the explosion of tools such as Claude Cowork, which made refining the text with AI all the more compelling as we were learning the power of these burgeoning tools at the same time as writing about them.

It is worth being clear about what AI did and did not do. It did not write this book. It did not determine the structure, develop the concepts, or create the use cases and examples throughout. What it did, however, was enhance the process. It made what could have been unstructured, complex, and time-consuming work simpler and more efficient. In many ways, this is exactly how we envision AI being used in law. That is, not as a replacement for human expertise and judgement, but as a tool that amplifies our capability to deliver high-quality work faster and more effectively.

A NOTE ON TERMINOLOGY

This book began its life as a book about generative AI. The term captured the technology that seized the legal profession's attention from late 2022 onwards, encompassing tools that could draft text, summarize documents, and answer questions in plain language. But the field has moved quickly, and the terminology has struggled to keep pace. The AI that matters to lawyers today goes well beyond generation: it includes agents that can execute multi-step workflows across different systems, protocols that connect AI models to firm data and tools, and new ways of building software that put development capabilities in the hands of non-engineers.

Trying to stretch 'generative AI' to cover all of this would be inaccurate as the tools are doing much more than just generating content. Attempting to introduce a new term for each development would be exhausting. This book therefore takes a pragmatic approach. We use 'AI' as the default term throughout. Where the distinction between generative AI, agentic AI, or any other specific form of the technology matters, we say so explicitly. Where it does not, 'AI' serves as the umbrella. Readers who have come to this book expecting a guide to generative AI should know that they are getting something broader, because the profession's needs are already broader than that single term can capture.

ACKNOWLEDGEMENTS

Finally, we want to thank the colleagues who took the time to read an early version of this book and give us their feedback: Tom Baldwin, Catherine Bamford, Paul Greenwood, Alicia Hardy, Matt McConnell, Jeff Rovner, Nikki Shaver, Catriona Wolfenden, and Horace Wu. We would also like to thank Luke Powell at Macfarlanes for granting permission for the firm's inclusion as a case study.

CHAPTER 1

What Is Changing and Why It Matters

THE AI LANDSCAPE IN LAW

How We Got Here

The legal profession has been following the same familiar path for decades. While new technologies have come and gone – each promising large-scale disruption – the scenery has remained recognizable. Law firms bill by the hour. In-house teams are often seen as cost centres. Partnership structures remain largely intact. Technology within firms is usually managed by centralized teams, while in-house teams generally have to rely on tools available across the rest of their business instead of having access to legal-specific solutions.

And yet, something feels different this time.

The ground is shifting. The billable hour remains, but clients are specifically asking about a definition of value that goes beyond the hours that a task takes, and they are unwilling to pay for tasks that could and should be supported (or supplanted) by technology. Alternative billing methods are on the rise. In-house legal teams are leveraging opportunities to become more strategic. Private capital investment in law is driving a review of partnership structures. AI-native law firms are being founded and funded at a breakneck pace. Lawyers are independently creating their own technology solutions without writing a single line of traditional code.

The pressure points have moved. The desire for change is coming not just from legal teams or innovators, but from the business world as a whole. In-house legal departments are deploying the same AI platforms as their outside counsel, and they can now benchmark outside counsel firm efficiency against their own capabilities and, in some instances, replace them. Investment in technology is at an all-time high as people expect its more widespread use.[1] Technology is delivering on things that have previously been overpromised and underdelivered in other hype cycles. End-users can interact with tools in natural language, reducing the barrier to entry. Something *has* changed, even if much of the ecosystem has not yet fully responded.

This chapter is about that change. It is about what is happening, why it is happening now, and why it matters for anyone working in or alongside the legal profession. We will examine where we are today, where we might be going, and how we get there, all through the lenses of evolution in technology, people, processes, and policy.

AI did not arrive in a vacuum. By the time large language models entered mainstream professional consciousness, the legal sector was already under sustained pressure to do more with less. To a large extent, AI has accelerated trends that were already underway rather than creating trends from scratch.

The Current Landscape

What is new is not simply the availability of technology, but the ways in which it can be used. A significant barrier to adoption in the past has been lawyers' inability to find time to use new technology. A new software system inevitably meant mastering new processes, menus, and user interfaces, and having to fit the way that lawyers work into the strictures of the particular tool. These tools also existed as a series of point solutions rather than as an integrated end-to-end workflow, despite the best efforts of vendors, meaning that users might have to jump through multiple interfaces, all with their own novel access points and user experiences.

But now lawyers are able to query the technology and ask for what they want using natural language. For senior lawyers in particular, the way that they prompt an AI tool may be no different to how they might give instructions to junior lawyers. This has been both a boon and a curse to the rapid expansion of generative AI: it has allowed people to pick up the tools and use them with little training, but it has led to less traction for more sophisticated uses of the technology.[2]

In these early years of the rise of generative AI, many tools suffered from the same pitfalls as previous technologies. The legal-specific AI tools that were created started out as simple chat-bot-style environments that were good at completing singular tasks. As the requirements for complexity grew, the tools added new features such as standardized tabular review, practice-specific workflows, and collaborative spaces. These all existed within environments that included new menus and new processes that went beyond simply typing in what you want the tool to do. For the most part, usage continued to focus on the simple chatbot environment. Lawyers may have wanted to do more, but they did not have time to learn the rapidly changing products without robust support from innovation teams (or, in the case of in-house counsel, from their IT or legal operations teams).

Enter agents. For the purposes of this book, the term 'agent' refers to an autonomous AI software system that can navigate between different environments in order to achieve a task. Until the introduction of agents, most AI tools consisted of a series of singular tasks that the technology would perform. Some people may have built bespoke workflows, but these tended to be templated prompts rather than true agents.

Let us take due diligence as a good example of an area in which agents can make a significant difference. In our example,

Company A is considering purchasing Company B. Company A has instructed Roscoe, Jasper & Mills LLP (RJM) to conduct a review of the status of Company B to highlight any potential legal risks before purchase. RJM is going to use its AI solution to support this due diligence. The corporate practice will coordinate the due diligence, but it will work with other practices that will be looking for potential issues in their specialist areas, such as employment or real estate. In the earliest examples of AI-enabled due diligence, a common flow might look like the following.

(1) Download the relevant documents regarding Company B from a data room.
(2) Create a new workspace within the generative AI tool.
(3) Upload the data room documents into the tool.
(4) Manually create a separate tabular review of the documents for each practice (e.g. corporate, employment, etc.), entering in the relevant prompts for each column.
(5) Select which documents belong to which table.
(6) Manually review the outputs by comparing them with the original documents.
(7) Ask the generative AI tool to produce a first draft due diligence report summarizing the main issues.

It is easy to see the opportunities for losing engagement from lawyers at each step. In order to benefit from the process, they would need to know how to upload documents into the tool, create new workspaces, set up a tabular review, enter in the appropriate prompts, and ask in a separate area of the tool to produce a written report. This does not look as straightforward as just telling the technology what you want it to do in plain language. With the assistance of an agent, however, this process can be much simpler.

(1) A lawyer from RJM writes a prompt saying that they wish to conduct a due diligence process and that they need a table of issues that creates a due diligence report.

(2) The agent completes the relevant steps to access the data room, create a workspace, categorize the documents, create the tables, write the prompts, and draft the due diligence report.

The first wave of AI felt revelatory because it was so simple. You could brief the tool like a junior and get work back. Then came the complexity of prompt chains, custom workflows, and multistep setups, each one another place to lose the thread. Agents close the loop. This second wave restores that original simplicity, with the tools now navigating an environment of systems on your behalf to accomplish outcomes. This assumes that the tool has appropriate access to the various systems – such as the data room or the document repository – and that the foundational elements of the AI in terms of security and deployment have been met, but the process for use has become much easier.

In addition, lawyers are no longer only hearing about AI tools from innovation teams or conferences. They are seeing colleagues use it, and they are being asked by their clients and partners whether entire processes can be automated end-to-end. They are fielding client queries about what AI is doing behind the scenes, and whether it is reflected in engagement price, speed, quality, and scope.

A SNAPSHOT: EVIDENCE FROM THE 'SKILLS' GENERATIVE AI USE CASES SURVEY

The pace of change makes it difficult to anchor our discussion in any specific tools or use cases. But experimentation is happening everywhere, often without central coordination, and often driven by individuals trying to solve immediate problems under time and cost pressure.

The SKILLS (Strategic Knowledge & Innovation Legal Leaders' Summit) questionnaire is an annual survey that polls leaders in the knowledge management and innovation community about the state of technology, AI, and knowledge management in their organizations.[3] The 2026 results provide a snapshot of how legal professionals use technology and how they intend to use it going forward. It is a useful look at a moment in time, designed to be revisited and compared against future iterations as the profession evolves. This year's responses highlight where AI tools are gaining traction across core legal workflows.

The results reveal gaps that are as important as the strengths. While respondents consistently assume technical legal expertise across their organizations, confidence drops when questions turn to process, data, technology, and change management expertise. While many respondents recognize the importance of these skills, a smaller number feel that they are supported, rewarded, or measured on them. The survey data also shows that organizations are moving beyond experimentation and into deployment and integration, and the important questions are no longer about trials or pilots, but about scale, governance, risk, and business impact.

The survey reveals telling priorities. When asked what legal professionals are currently working on, the top responses cluster around strategy, AI policy, AI training, and deploying internal AI capabilities. Taken together, these responses reveal a profession finishing off the foundational work of getting 'AI-ready'. When asked what they want to learn and talk about in the coming year, the answers shift towards practical application, agentic workflows, and client collaboration portals. This gap between current focus and desired knowledge suggests a profession that has moved beyond whether to adopt AI and is now grappling with how to deploy it effectively and – following quickly on the heels of that – how to calculate time and cost savings. The results dashboard will continue to be updated over time, allowing readers to see how opinions shift and change.[4]

WHY IS CHANGE HAPPENING: THE PEOPLE

One way of understanding what is changing is to look not at technology first, but at people. AI is empowering individuals to work in ways that were not previously possible. The ability to produce a complex output with AI means that smaller firms can go up against firms that have previously set themselves apart by being able to throw large numbers of people at a problem. It means that in-house teams can do the work (or at least some of the work) that outside counsel would have done in the past. It means that individual lawyers can create solutions by 'vibe coding' (see chapter 9) that would have only previously been possible by procuring software or leveraging a development team.

In-house legal departments have become increasingly sophisticated. Major corporations are now deploying the same AI platforms as their outside counsel, and they are using them to build internal capabilities. AI is arguably much easier to deploy in-house, where the types of activity being undertaken are more repeatable and consistent. Consider an AI platform that is designed to review a contract against a playbook (that is, a guide containing the rules, preferred clauses, fallback positions, and limits on acceptable negotiations for a legal team). In an in-house team, that platform considers each of the contracts against a single playbook. In a law firm, the playbook used depends on the practice, the client, and – in the case of large global firms – the jurisdiction and country. In a firm, deployment and use of some of the most useful features becomes much more complex.

When both sides have access to the same tools, the differentiators become the knowledge and judgement that sit on top of those tools. There are now countless instances of clients giving their law firms a 'first pass' review that has been conducted by AI and asking outside counsel to confirm or amend the output. Reliance on outside counsel has not disappeared: they can provide their expertise gleaned from conducting many of the same types of activity for other clients, and, of course, they are insured should anything go wrong. But updating a first pass review, or even creating one in the event that doing so is left to the firm, does not take anywhere near as long as providing advice from first principles. In a profession that is built on the billable hour, this means that clients are expecting savings.

As well as clients, lawyers themselves are driving change. Some no longer want to – or feel that they can – conduct certain types of work manually. A lot of the push in this area is coming either from juniors who are joining law firms and expecting to encounter the same technologies they use in their daily lives or from lateral hires joining from more technologically advanced teams. There is an expectation that the teams they are joining will already use AI. There is also a drive from more senior lawyers who are seeking to lower their reliance on overly expensive junior lawyers as a result of pressure from their clients.

The other faction driving this change is leadership. In law firms, leaders sensing the direction of travel are making the use of AI a fundamental part of lawyer development, and they are driving AI usage through a range of means.[5] Meanwhile, business leaders, who have already been asking in-house teams to be more efficient for years, are asking for greater speed and more capability from their lawyers.

This matters because change does not happen magically. Change is driven by people and pressure, and the pressure to be more efficient is now coming from multiple directions at once. Yet the question of what efficiency *actually* means remains unresolved. If a task that once took ten hours now takes two, does the lawyer do five times as many tasks or does the organization need fewer lawyers? How should the law firm charge for that work? The answers are still far from clear. This uncertainty creates anxiety across the profession, but these questions certainly cannot be ignored.

WHY CHANGE IS HAPPENING: THE ECONOMIC REALITY

If there is a single thread that runs through almost every conversation about change in law, it is cost. In-house legal teams are being squeezed. They are being asked to move closer to the business, to be more strategic, and to demonstrate value in ways that go beyond technical accuracy. At the same time, their budgets are under scrutiny, often more intensely than for other professional functions.

For years, we heard about 'the death of the billable hour' and about how clients would like things to change and for legal work to be less expensive. In reality, the opposite has happened. Partners at top law firms are taking home much more money than they used to a decade ago. But why? The answer lies in the law of supply and demand. Leaving aside the conversation about a protective guild and other barriers to entry, the reality is that law firms have been able to resist the demand for change because of relatively limited supply.

But now both sides of the supply and demand equation are shifting. Using AI, law firms can produce more with the same number of lawyers, while at the same time, clients are expected to adopt AI in-house and use their outside counsel less often.

Pressure in the legal services ecosystem does not stay put. Each participant that feels it exerts it on the next. When clients are pressed on cost and efficiency, they press their outside counsel. When firms are pressed by their clients, they press their vendors, their pricing models, and their own people. New 'AI-first' law firms have entered the market,[6] providing yet another option for clients looking to diversify their panels beyond traditional law firms, especially for high-volume work.

The question is no longer simply 'Are you good lawyers?' but 'Are you the *right* lawyers, at the *right* price, delivering the *right* outcomes?' Over all of this looms the monolith that has so far remained unchanged in the traditional law firm model: the billable hour. It is no secret that lawyers bill by the hour (or by six-minute segments if you want to be exact). There has always been a tension between this billing model and the rapid advancement of technologies that increase the speed of tasks. If lawyers are paid by the hour, why would they ever prioritize efficiency? But, for the first time, we are seeing the foundations of the billable hour begin to crumble.

Alternative fee arrangements have become more common, but they are still far from the norm. Fixed fees, capped fees, and blended rates appear to promise improved predictability. At the same time, some clients are becoming more sophisticated in how they buy legal services, requiring secondments or innovation projects to be bundled into fee arrangements, effectively shifting risk and experimentation onto their advisors. Some clients have gone further, implementing credit systems that tie fees to demonstrable efficiency gains. If a firm fails to deliver, the client might claw back a portion of fees at year-end. Others are asking firms to demonstrate the 'delts', or the difference between what the work cost before AI and what it should cost now. Firms must be able to adequately demonstrate this delta (and understand what it means for the business model) because the era of trusting that outside counsel will pass on efficiency gains voluntarily appears to be at an end, at least for some.

All these factors have led to much more discussion of 'value', and this movement makes sense. Consider a due diligence exercise like the one in our earlier example. If that exercise used to take ten hours and now only takes one, then RJM is going to lose nine-tenths of its revenue for the exercise. To bolster that revenue, it could now do more matters of this type, but there are only so many company acquisitions happening at once. On the other hand, what is the value to Company A of completing a purchase of a company faster? It is not just the reduced legal spend. The value is in how much more quickly they can start trading with their newly purchased Company B. Clearly, that is also worth something.

So how do we reach a middle ground? Value-based pricing seeks to find a compromise between the traditional hours model and the benefits to the client of more efficient work, while still recognizing the time and expertise of the law firm (as well as the insurance protection it provides). Compare this with a mechanic who might charge a premium price for fixing a fault in a car. While the fix might only take the mechanic ten minutes, you are not paying solely for their time: you are paying for the years of expertise that allowed them to solve your problem in ten minutes, allowing you to get back on the road much sooner. That is where the pricing of legal matters is moving as AI becomes more prevalent.

Changing existing processes and working practices takes time, however, and there is a growing unwillingness from clients to pay for work that feels non-billable (such as training), for perceived internal inefficiencies, or for duplicated effort. This is a difficult quandary for law firms that have to incentivize their lawyers to experiment and optimize workflows for efficiency while clients refuse to pay for that innovation.

The billable hour is also still the primary metric for *rewarding* lawyers within firms (and in some in-house teams). This generally translates into lawyers hitting a certain number of hours to qualify for a bonus. There has been some change to this core structure in recent years, with the introduction of forms of 'innovation hours' or 'knowledge hours' that contribute towards the hours target, but the core model has largely remained unchanged. Some firms are making AI usage part of work appraisals, reviews, and even discussions around bonuses. For now, however, the system publicly celebrates change and innovation while privately rewarding continuity.

TIME, TRANSPARENCY, AND THE METRICS PROBLEM

Charging for or rewarding time is not the only consideration. As has been noted, expectations have changed. Clients now simply expect answers faster. Lawyers expect tools to remove friction. Everyone feels busier, even when technology promises efficiency. Clients increasingly want transparency; they want to know what they are paying for, how long it will take, and what they will get. Firms want flexibility, discretion, and protection against risk. This has forced more conversations within the profession focused on what actually counts as a valuable key performance indicator. Hours billed are easy to measure, but they are a poor proxy for value in a world where pricing is more like the mechanic example above.

Even where clients use alternative fee arrangements, there is still an expectation of a series of narratives showing the activities undertaken by the lawyers. This is understandable: clients want value for money, and in a system where hours have always been the primary metric, asking to see what was done during those hours is a logical request. The problem is how to keep that level of transparency when pricing on value. Does the law firm showcase its years of expertise? Do clients start to rank their firms with net promoter scores? Will we we start to see law firm comparison sites where clients can choose a firm based on the best price?[7] Does the industry become more reliant on the success of individual practitioners of law rather than on the firm as a whole? These questions can no longer be avoided, but there are no easy answers.

Metrics for internal assessments are an equally difficult proposition. If we accept that tracking hours drives inefficiency, then what alternative should be tracked instead? The number of prompts in an AI system does not guarantee *good* usage. Innovation contributions, process improvements, and collaboration are harder to quantify – and, therefore, easier to ignore.

WHY CHANGE IS HAPPENING: COMPETITION, REGULATION, AND NEW MARKET DYNAMICS

Cost and expectation pressures alone do not explain the scale of change. Competition has intensified, not just between law firms but between entirely different models of legal service delivery. In England and Wales, alternative business structures (ABSs) have been in existence since 2012, following the introduction of the Legal Services Act 2007. These allow non-lawyers to own and invest in legal businesses. In the United States, regulatory change has been slower and more fragmented, but experimentation is increasing. While the initial promise of ABSs was to revolutionize the market in England and Wales, the effect has mostly been felt at the fringes of the core legal market. What they have done is cause clients to diversify their panels: what was previously a collection of law firms will now almost always include either an ABS or a law firm that is able to conduct ABS-style work, which tends to be higher-volume work with consistent pricing. What this change has proved is that clients are more willing to look beyond the traditional partnership model if doing so delivers value.

The change in the United States, however, is coming at a different time. Lawyer and technologist Damien Riehl suggests that with the use of AI, 'the unauthorized practice of law statutes might die, not with a bang, but with a whimper – through regulatory non-enforcement'.[8]

The 'regulatory non-enforcement' Riehl talks about relates to the fact that, either directly or indirectly, the unauthorized practice of law is going to involve the biggest companies in the world: Google, Microsoft, OpenAI, Anthropic, and Meta (and possibly others). While individual users may be the ones generating legal outputs, the underlying automation technology is controlled by these companies, making meaningful enforcement politically and economically difficult.

In practice, many AI-first legal services companies in the United States have found a structural workaround through the 'managed services organization' (MSO) model. Under this structure, a technology company provides the platform, the back-office operations, and the AI infrastructure, while a separately owned, lawyer-controlled entity delivers the legal services. The arrangement satisfies unauthorized-practice rules on paper while enabling a fundamentally different operating model – one in which the technology company, not the law firm, is the primary driver of how work gets done.

The proliferation of automated workflows means that tasks that once required lawyer oversight are now performed by software, with a paralegal, perhaps, pushing a button. Is this the practice of law? That question is increasingly difficult to answer, and perhaps it is increasingly irrelevant. What matters is that work is moving, often invisibly, away from traditional providers. Look at the UK property conveyancing market, where the majority of work is completed by individuals who are not qualified lawyers. For work that is repeatable and subject to strict rules with little scope for complex interpretation, it is easy to see why clients might not care if the person 'pushing the button' is or is not a lawyer.

With the diversification of outside counsel panels, new entrants are more specialized. The result is not simply more competition, but *different* competition, forcing law firms and legal teams to articulate what makes them distinct. Large firms that once competed on their ability to staff matters with dozens of associates now find that advantage eroding. Smaller, more agile competitors can produce comparable output with AI assistance, at lower cost.

These include new 'AI-first' law firms. In the United Kingdom this started with the Solicitors Regulation Authority approving Garfield.Law Limited,[9] which uses an AI-powered litigation assistant to help recover unpaid debts. Other entrants have followed, such as LawFairy, which uses what could be described as a more traditional deterministic AI solution rather than a probabilistic one.[10] There are other examples of 'hybrid' AI firms, and although at present they are exclusively used in areas that deal with high-volume, rules-based work, they show potential to disrupt the profession in these areas.

Perhaps most significant is the role of legal technology vendors themselves. Platforms that began as tools are increasingly hiring Big Law lawyers, building client relationships, selling to in-house teams, and developing the expertise to deliver legal work directly. They already have the software and they are acquiring the knowledge; what remains is regulatory permission. Many of these legal-technology AI companies have multimillion-dollar valuations, and it is hard to see how those valuations can be justified if they remain only technology vendors who sell into law firms. Whether these vendors become law firms, acquire law firms, or create new hybrid structures remains to be seen, but there is a clear direction of travel, with one observer calling these vendors 'the biggest Trojan Horse in legal'.

A POSSIBLE FUTURE

The legal profession finds itself at a point where technology, people, economic factors, and policy are all shifting at once. And it is not just in legal that this is happening. Almost every profession is experiencing this shift. None of these changes can be understood in isolation. AI matters not because it is novel, but because it collides with existing pressures in a system that is already stretched thin. Movement is beginning, but the real question is one of where we are going.

What might the future look like? There are a number of possibilities around where the legal profession could end up, but it is helpful to look at the most extreme versions. An example we will return to throughout the book is one that can best be described as 'legal streaming' or 'law as a service' (LaaS). Consider a world in which law is more akin to the world of streaming services. Law firms, legal publishers, sole practitioners, and other knowledge providers 'broadcast' their services into platform providers. They might do this from their own environments or by streaming to a 'box' through which a client can utilize these services. Clients can then subscribe to the services they want and embed them into their own systems as needed. This means a client who has to do a due diligence exercise might activate their 'due diligence agent'. The parts of this agentic workflow might use one firm's mergers and acquisitions law 'channel' for their corporate assessment of the risks of the purchase, while using another firm's employment law 'channel' for the employment aspects and yet another's real estate 'channel'. The agent would navigate between these specialists to give a holistic overview of the potential legal issues. Playbooks, precedents, deal analytics, and advisory services flow through a single interface, accessible on demand. This is an interesting – if extreme – vision to consider.[11]

How do you prepare for the various possibilities of the future? We have already established that change is happening quickly and that no one knows exactly what the profession will look like, but if you do the groundwork, that work will not be wasted. Understand where your data is, what the single points of truth are, and whether the data is clean and structured. You will not regret taking the time to understand the key processes and tasks that your organization undertakes, or where those processes might be made more efficient. And you will see benefits immediately for training your people to think differently about their work and to be curious and aware of whether the things they are doing can be done more efficiently and effectively.

The next chapters will explore how these pressures play out in practice; how individuals respond; how organizations attempt to regain control; and how governance, incentives, and culture shape what is possible.

A key point to remember is that the ground has moved. Standing still is no longer an option. And the decisions made in response to this moment will shape not just how law is practised, but who gets to practise it, and on what terms.

IN PRACTICE

In a Sentence

The ground under the profession has moved. Pressure on pricing, people, competition, and regulation is arriving all at once, and the cost of standing still is no longer neutral.

What to Remember

» AI only highlighted pressures that were already building in the profession. The billable hour model, demands on in-house teams, and client requests for transparency all predate the 'GPT moment'.

- Clients are now benchmarking outside counsel against their own in-house AI capability. The question has moved from 'Are you good lawyers?' to 'Are you the right lawyers, at the right price, for the right outcome?'
- The future of the profession is still being written, but the foundations are already clear: clean data, mapped processes, and people curious about new ways of working.

What to Do with This

- Consider the four commercial pressures of people, economics, competition, and regulation. Which can you most easily affect right now? That is where the work starts.
- Audit where your matter data lives, whether it is clean, and who owns it. That work pays off in every future discussed in the rest of this book.
- Treat standing still as a choice with consequences, not a safe default. The decisions you make (or avoid) at this moment matter.

Questions to Sit With

- If a client handed you a first-pass AI review of a contract tomorrow and asked you to confirm it, what would you bill them for, and could you defend the number?
- Where in your organization is pressure for change coming from? If your answer is 'nowhere yet', is that because it is not coming or because you are not looking?

CHAPTER 2

How It Works

...AND WHY LAWYERS SHOULD UNDERSTAND IT

Every time the legal profession encounters a major technological shift, the same question surfaces. To what extent should lawyers become experts in the technology? With AI, the question has become whether lawyers should be legal engineers, or be able to fully understand and explain neural networks, or be able to learn to build bespoke products themselves. The short answer is that while it is unlikely that every lawyer will, or should, become a technical expert, they do need to understand what the technology does and how it intersects with their work. The common refrain is that lawyers will be replaced not by AI but by another lawyer using AI. There is truth in that, even if the timeline remains uncertain.

AI tools are already embedded in everyday legal work and have been for some time. Research platforms, document review systems, eDiscovery tools, and productivity assistants all rely on some form of artificial intelligence. Headlines now proclaim AI's ability to draft contracts,[1] summarize case law,[2] predict litigation outcomes,[3] and build software tools.[4] Lawyers do not need to become computer scientists to use these tools well, but a working understanding of the underlying technology helps ensure it is used appropriately, safely, and with some creativity.

Despite the rapid adoption and considerable discussion, genuine misunderstanding persists about what artificial intelligence actually is and how it works. This leads to lawyers not using AI correctly, not using it at all, or expecting it to do things for which it is not well suited and being disappointed when it falls short. All of these stand in the way of AI being fully integrated into how law is practised.

This chapter does not attempt a comprehensive history of artificial intelligence. The history would fill several volumes and the technology continues to evolve rapidly. Instead, it traces the milestones in AI development that matter most to the legal profession; explains how the technology actually works; identifies what it is good at; and introduces the directions the profession is heading via agents, protocols, and new ways of building software. Some used to define AI as 'anything that we needed a human to do yesterday, and computers can do now', but that definition does not cover all the new capabilities that go beyond what a human could ever do.

As discussed in 'A Note on Terminology' in our preface, generative AI is a broad category that includes systems capable of generating text, images, audio, video, and code. This chapter focuses primarily on the evolution of the text-centric systems that are most directly relevant to legal work. Other modalities are developing quickly, but it is chiefly language models that are reshaping how lawyers draft, research, analyse, and advise.

MILESTONES IN AI THAT MATTER FOR LAW

The story of artificial intelligence stretches back more than seventy years, but not all of it is equally relevant to the practice of law. What follows are five developments that have had, or are having, the most direct impact on how legal work is performed. The first four are covered in this section. The fifth – the emergence of AI agents – warrants its own treatment later in the chapter, once the mechanics of generative AI have been established. When examining these milestones, the goal is to provide enough context to understand where today's tools came from and why they work the way they do.

The evolution of legal technology is a story of natural language processing (NLP) applied to law. This is the specific branch of artificial intelligence dedicated to the interaction between computers and human language.[5] While early legal AI attempted to 'solve' language through logic and rigid rules, the field has shifted towards models that can handle the inherent ambiguity and context dependency of the law. Understanding the milestones below requires seeing them as a progression in how NLP systems 'read' and 'understand' text.

Milestone 1: Rule-Based Systems and the First Attempt to Codify Legal Reasoning

The earliest attempts to apply AI in legal settings were rule-based systems. Beginning in the 1950s, computer scientists explored whether machines could replicate aspects of human reasoning by encoding knowledge directly as rules. If a certain condition occurred, the program would respond in a predetermined way. At their core, these systems were akin to advanced 'choose your own adventure' novels.[6]

For the legal profession, this was the first time anyone had tried to put legal decision-making into software. If a contract contains a certain clause, flag it. If a regulatory filing is missing a particular element, alert the user. These early tools found their way into compliance checking and basic document assembly, and for straightforward, rules-driven tasks they provided real value.

But they struggled to scale. The world is too complex to be captured entirely through explicit rules, and this was especially true for legal work, where the answer to most questions is 'it depends'. While the clause you are looking for might sometimes be labelled exactly as the technology is expecting, across the wide number of document types, house styles, and jurisdiction-specific nuances, the titles and the content can often shift enough to confuse the software.

Many legal technologists have spent years acting as translators between two professional cultures. Developers need strict, step-by-step logic; lawyers reason contextually, conditionally, and with exceptions at every turn.

Interest in AI rose and fell in cycles often referred to as 'AI summers' and 'AI winters'. The technology was promising but the gap between what it could do and what the profession needed remained wide.

Milestone 2: Machine Learning and the Transformation of Document Review

The milestone that most changed how lawyers worked, day to day, was the rise of machine learning. Instead of programming computers with explicit rules, researchers began training models to identify patterns within data. By analysing large datasets, these systems could learn statistical relationships and use them to make predictions or classifications. The shift from 'tell the computer exactly what to look for' to 'show the computer examples and let it learn' was profound.

For the legal profession, the impact was most immediately felt in discovery and document review. Technology-assisted review (TAR) and predictive coding allowed review platforms to codify a lawyer's initial decisions and classifications and then apply those patterns across thousands or millions of documents. Instead of hand-coding rules about what made a document privileged or relevant, the system could learn from examples. This was a sea change for litigation and discovery, reducing the time and cost of review by orders of magnitude in some cases.

Machine learning also powered fraud-detection tools, contract analytics, and early forms of legal research assistants. Many lawyers used these technologies without knowing they were 'using AI'. But TAR, more than any other application, was the moment that AI stopped being a theoretical proposition for the legal profession and started being something that affected how matters were staffed, priced, and run.

The leap from machine learning to modern generative AI was made possible by a further development called deep learning. Deep learning is a specialized subset of machine learning that uses neural networks: multilayered mathematical structures that allow a model to process information in a way that captures complex relationships within data. This shift from simple statistical correlations to deep neural architectures is what paved the way for AI to 'pay attention' to context across entire documents, thereby setting the stage for the next breakthrough.

Milestone 3: Transformers and the Leap to Large Language Models

The AI tools that lawyers use today – the ones that can draft memos, summarize case law, and answer questions in plain language – exist because of a specific technical breakthrough. The 'transformer' architecture was introduced in 2017 in a paper titled 'Attention Is All You Need', written by Ashish Vaswani and colleagues at Google,[7] and this is the next milestone in the story of AI in the legal profession.

The contrast with what came before makes the breakthrough clearer. Earlier language models could represent words as numerical vectors and identify relationships between them, famously capturing, for example, that 'king minus man plus woman equals queen'.[8] While this improved search, the models could not understand context. Knowing that 'termination clause' and 'exit provision' are related is not the same as knowing which one applies in a given sentence. Transformers solved that problem.

Instead of processing text word by word in sequence, a transformer could look at entire sentences and paragraphs at once, weighing how each word relates to every other word.

This mechanism, called 'attention', is what allows modern AI to handle the ambiguity that saturates legal language. Consider the word 'bank'. Among other things, it could mean a financial institution, the side of a river, or the act of relying on something. When a transformer encounters 'bank' in 'the client's funds were held at the bank pending regulatory approval', it pays attention to the words 'client', 'funds', and 'regulatory' to determine the correct meaning. Legal documents are full of terms whose meaning depends on context. 'Consideration', 'execution', 'charge', and 'assignment' are all good examples. The transformer architecture is what allows AI systems to handle this kind of interpretive work.[9]

The transformer opened the door to two families of models that now underpin most legal AI tools. In June 2018 OpenAI introduced GPT-1, a model trained to predict the next word in a sequence.[10] Given the beginning of a sentence, it learned what word should follow by processing vast amounts of text. A few months later, in October 2018, Google introduced BERT.[11] Where GPT read text in one direction, BERT took a different approach: it masked roughly 15% of the words in a passage and trained the model to predict the missing words using context from both sides. This made BERT particularly effective at understanding and classifying text. For legal technology, BERT improved document classification, entity recognition, and semantic search in ways that earlier models could not match. GPT, when scaled up with billions of parameters, became capable of generating coherent, contextually appropriate text across a wide range of topics. Both had applications to the legal profession.

Milestone 4: The ChatGPT Moment

The release of ChatGPT on 30 November 2022 was, for the legal profession, a milestone in its own right. The underlying technology had been developing for years, but ChatGPT was the moment it became tangible. Within five days the tool had over a million users.[12] Within two months it had 100 million, making it the fastest-growing consumer software application in history at the time of its launch.[13] Although our focus is on the legal profession, law does not exist in a vacuum. ChatGPT quickly permeated the personal lives of lawyers and the businesses of their clients, becoming ubiquitous to the same degree as emails had earlier but on a significantly reduced timescale.

For lawyers, this was the first time many practitioners had seen generative AI in action, and they began to consider what it meant for their work. What had been a research curiosity became something you could type into and get a plausible legal memo back from. Partners who had never engaged with legal technology suddenly had opinions about AI. Clients started asking what AI was doing behind the scenes. Chief Executive Officers and Chief Operating Officers were questioning whether legal teams could use it to reduce headcount or reliance on external counsel. Associates began experimenting on their own. Innovation teams that had spent years trying to get attention for legal technology initiatives found themselves fielding more requests than they could handle.

The ChatGPT moment did not create new capabilities so much as make existing ones visible and accessible. But visibility matters. It forced conversations about pricing, staffing, training, and risk that legal firms had been putting off. The legal profession's relationship with AI divides into the time before ChatGPT and the time after it.

To understand why ChatGPT felt so different from the tools that came before it, it helps to look under the hood at the statistical engine that drives the text. It is worth noting that while OpenAI and Google's BERT were first to market, Anthropic's Claude, Google's Gemini, and Meta's LLaMA are also now major forces powering legal AI.

The fifth and most recent milestone, the emergence of AI agents, builds on everything covered so far, so we will return to it later in the chapter once we have looked under the hood at how generative AI actually works.

HOW GENERATIVE AI ACTUALLY WORKS

Tokens and Context Windows

Instead of processing language as words, large language models break text down into tokens, which are small units that may represent a word, part of a word, or a piece of punctuation. One token represents roughly four characters or three-quarters of a word, though this varies by language and tokenizer. Most modern models use a subword tokenization method that splits text into these smaller units based on patterns learned from training data. When a prompt is entered, the model converts the text into tokens and processes those tokens as numerical representations. It then predicts the next token in the sequence based on probability distributions learned during training.

A related concept is the context window. This refers to the total number of tokens the model can hold in working memory at one time, and it must contain both the input and the output. A model with a context window of 100,000 tokens has to fit the material you feed in and the response it generates within that token budget. Both share the same finite space. If a conversation grows too long or too much information is included, earlier material falls outside the window and is effectively forgotten. For legal workflows that involve large datasets or for complex matters with many documents, this constraint is worth keeping in mind.

Hallucinations and the Probabilistic Nature of AI

Generative AI can appear to be almost magical. A user types a question into a chat interface and receives a detailed response within seconds. It is tempting to assume the system 'understands' the question in the same way a human would, particularly when we anthropomorphize our tools by giving them human names.

In reality, the underlying mechanism is statistical rather than cognitive. Large language models are trained on vast collections of text drawn from books, articles, websites, and other sources. During training, the model learns to predict the most likely next word in a sequence given the words that came before it. When a user enters a prompt, the model does not, for the most part, retrieve an answer from a database or search engine, but rather it generates a response token by token, selecting each word based on probabilities derived from its training.

This process is stochastic, meaning it involves probabilities rather than deterministic rules. Ask the same question twice and you may get slightly different answers, because multiple responses could plausibly follow the same prompt.

There is also the problem – encountered particularly in the early days of the technology – of these tools not being designed to *be* correct but to *sound* correct. That distinction matters enormously in a profession built on accuracy. Although they are no longer surprising stories, in the early days incidents involving 'hallucinations' attracted significant press attention. These fictional citations happen when AI systems generate information that appears plausible but is incorrect or entirely fabricated. As some of the lawyers involved in one of the earliest widely reported cases wrote in their defence, 'We made a good-faith mistake in failing to believe that a piece of technology could be making up cases out of whole cloth.'[14]

A hallucination occurs when the model generates text based on statistical patterns instead of verifying facts against an authoritative source. The model has no intrinsic mechanism for assessing the truth of its own output. It may produce answers that are internally consistent but actually wrong. For lawyers, this is a critical concern. Legal work depends on accuracy, verifiable sources, and careful interpretation of authoritative texts. The response to the problem is not, though, to avoid AI altogether but to recognize its role. Generative AI is often best used either as a drafting and analytical assistant, producing initial outputs that a professional then reviews and verifies, or as a sparring partner or second pair of eyes for existing content. It should be treated as a capable tool and not as an autonomous advisor.

For lawyers accustomed to working with structured sources such as statutes and precedents, the probabilistic approach can be counterintuitive. Consider document automation, for example. AI tools are increasingly used to fill in templates or automate documents, and a lawyer might reasonably wonder why they need both a document automation tool and AI when the latter seems to do the same thing. The answer is that the probabilistic nature of generative AI means it will not always produce the same results. This is a significant problem when it comes to structured legal documents and templates where consistency matters.

Catherine Bamford, founder of BamLegal and one of the more rigorous practitioners working at the intersection of law and document automation, draws a useful distinction here. She argues that lawyers will ultimately rely on a combination of two approaches: 'AI to extract info, context and intent'; and 'deterministic logic to produce something consistent, trusted and risk free'.[15] The two approaches are complementary, not competing.

CONNECTING AI TO REAL INFORMATION

Generative AI tools are trained on general datasets and do not automatically have access to specific information such as a law firm's internal knowledge base or a client's documents. To address this, many systems use a technique called retrieval-augmented generation (RAG). The system first searches a dataset or knowledge base for relevant information. It converts the original query into a numerical format, compares it against an index of available knowledge, retrieves matching material, and provides that material to the language model as part of the prompt so it can generate a response grounded in those sources. A legal research AI assistant, for instance, might retrieve relevant cases or legislation from a database before generating a summary. This reduces the risk of hallucinations and ensures the model's output is anchored in actual documents rather than statistical guesswork.

It is worth noting that the relationship between RAG and context windows is shifting. When context windows were small, RAG was the only practical way to get large volumes of firm-specific data into a model. But by 2026 several leading models offered context windows of a million tokens or more, which is roughly equivalent to 1,500–2,000 pages of text. This meant that lawyers using those tools could drop entire trial transcripts, large sets of discovery documents, or lengthy regulatory filings directly into a single prompt without needing a separate retrieval system. At the time of writing, RAG remains essential for searching across massive firm-wide databases where the relevant material is not known in advance, which is why the concept of enterprise search engines such as DeepJudge remains popular. But for tasks where the lawyer already knows which documents matter, long context windows have made it possible to skip the retrieval step entirely and work with the source material directly.

This also highlights the important point that AI is only as useful as the data it can access. In the early days of generative AI deployment within law firms, many lawyers asked internal AI tools questions about firm financials, client matters, or internal precedents. The tools could not answer because they were not connected to those datasets. One of the authors encountered another early and entertaining example of this when asking the legal AI tool Harvey, 'How does Harvey arrive at its answers?' The tool's response was to give an overview of why the Batman villain Two-Face, whose alter ego is Harvey Dent, made his decisions on the flip of a coin. Harvey did not have the data to understand that *it was* Harvey.

FIVE CORE CAPABILITIES

Modern AI tools can be grouped by their capabilities, and understanding these functions helps when evaluating what a particular product can and cannot do.

- *Prediction.* AI can analyse data and forecast outcomes. In a legal context, this might include estimating litigation risk or predicting the likelihood of certain contractual clauses appearing in a document.
- *Classification.* AI can categorize information based on patterns learned during training. Document review platforms frequently use this to identify privileged materials, relevant documents, or particular clause types during a due diligence exercise.
- *Extraction.* AI can pull specific pieces of information from unstructured text: key dates, party names, obligations, or financial figures from contracts or regulatory filings.
- *Generation.* AI can create new content. This includes drafting text, generating summaries, producing code, or answering questions in conversational language.
- *Reasoning.* AI can process complex problems step by step before delivering a final response. Unlike standard generative systems that predict the next token in a single pass, reasoning systems employ a 'chain-of-thought' mechanism to logically evaluate multiple possibilities and self-correct during generation. For lawyers, this allows for more reliable performance in high-stakes tasks such as synthesizing contradictory regulatory requirements, performing deep case law analysis, or identifying logical gaps in complex witness testimony.

Many modern tools combine these approaches. A legal AI platform might first classify documents, then extract key data points, then summarize the results, and finally generate insights for the user. Understanding where a tool falls in this taxonomy helps set realistic expectations about what it can deliver.

Beyond these individual capabilities lies the category of AI agents, which represent a fundamental shift from static tools to autonomous systems capable of stringing these different capabilities together. This category is discussed in 'The Emergence of AI Agents' below.

WHAT AI IS ACTUALLY GOOD AT

With the technical foundations covered, the practical question is what generative AI does well in legal work. The short answer is that it excels at tasks involving language transformation, i.e. taking language in one form and turning it into another. This includes drafting and redrafting text, summarizing long or complex documents, extracting key information from documents, and answering questions based on provided material.

Because legal work is heavily language based, many everyday tasks fall squarely into these categories. In practice, AI can assist with drafting the first version of a document, reviewing large sets of materials during eDiscovery and due diligence, producing summaries of case law, retrieving information from knowledge repositories, and preparing presentations and client briefings. Rather than replacing legal judgement, these capabilities accelerate the parts of the workflow that involve processing and organizing large amounts of information.

It is equally important to be honest about where the technology is less reliable. Tasks that require precise formatting or layout control remain difficult. AI can draft content well but does not always handle the mechanics of document formatting consistently. And while AI can provide useful commentary and analysis when looking at differences between documents, it is not a reliable replacement for purpose-built comparison tools, particularly when dealing with longer documents. These limitations are not fatal flaws. They are things to know so that the right tool gets used for the right job.

THE EMERGENCE OF AI AGENTS, THE FIFTH MILESTONE

Most early generative AI systems functioned as conversational interfaces. A user would submit a prompt, receive an answer, and then decide what to do next. The system itself did not take independent actions and could not string together a series of steps or reach into other systems. For a lawyer using one of these tools, every action was a discrete interaction. Ask a question, get an answer, copy the answer into a document, switch to another system, and repeat.

Agents change this fundamentally. As defined in chapter 1, an agent is an autonomous AI-powered system that can undertake a series of actions across different tools and environments to accomplish a goal. Given a brief, the agent works out what steps are needed, which tools to use, and in what order, and it then runs the sequence without waiting to be told what to do at each stage.

Consider how this applies to a practical legal workflow. A legal research agent might interpret a user's question, determine that it needs to search a legal database, retrieve and analyse the relevant cases, cross-reference those against internal precedent documents, and produce a summary memorandum. Each step involves interacting with a different external system. The agent decides the sequence and manages the handoffs between systems without requiring the user to orchestrate each step manually.

For legal teams, this is the shift from AI as a chatbot to AI as a colleague who can follow a multistep brief. Due diligence reviews, regulatory monitoring, knowledge retrieval, contract analysis, and internal research requests all involve multiple steps across multiple systems, and all of them are candidates for agentic workflows. The first wave of generative AI adoption in law was about doing individual tasks faster. Agents represent the second wave, where the tools move from completing discrete tasks to navigating an environment of tools to accomplish outcomes.

This does assume both that the agent has appropriate access to the various systems involved and that the foundational elements of security and deployment have been addressed. But the process for use becomes dramatically simpler. Where a lawyer once had to learn the menus, workflows, and interfaces of each separate tool, an agent can accept a brief in natural language and handle the rest. The skill for the lawyer becomes less about navigating software and more about articulating what you need and verifying what you get back.

MODEL CONTEXT PROTOCOL

For agents to work in practice, they need a structured way to communicate with external systems. A model can produce text on its own, but it does not know how to access a document repository, search a legal database, or pull information from a knowledge management system. Model Context Protocol (MCP), an open standard introduced by Anthropic in November 2024, provides that structure.

In simple terms, MCP is a standardized way of connecting an AI model to the tools and data sources it needs to do its work. Think of it like the connectors that allow different pieces of software to talk to each other, except MCP is designed specifically for AI systems that need to decide on the fly which tool to reach for. A law firm can define which systems are available and what data each can access, and it can then add new tools over time without rebuilding the underlying model. For legal teams, MCP is the plumbing that makes agents practical rather than theoretical.

The agentic and MCP capabilities described above have also begun to change how software itself is built via 'vibe coding'. Discussed in chapter 9, vibe coding is essentially the creation of software through conversational prompts rather than through traditional programming.

WHY LAWYERS SHOULD UNDERSTAND THE TECHNOLOGY

Some lawyers will ask whether they really need to understand any of this. After all, most professionals use technology without knowing how it works internally. But they do need to understand it. Similarly, there are senior practitioners who wonder whether they can 'wait it out' and avoid understanding AI until they retire. They cannot.

Unlike earlier legal software built for a single task, many modern AI tools are general purpose and can be applied to a wide range of problems. The user decides how the technology is used. This means that the value of the tool increasingly depends on the imagination and judgement of the professional using it, and that requires understanding what the tool can and cannot do.

Understanding the technology also helps lawyers assess risk and reliability. More and more often, lawyers are involved in decisions about procurement, governance, and regulation of AI systems. Clients expect their legal advisors to understand both the capabilities and the risks associated with these technologies. Basic technical literacy also enables more productive collaboration with the technologists and AI specialists who are becoming part of every legal team, just as lawyers have long worked alongside accountants, project managers, and data analysts.

UNDERSTANDING ENOUGH TO ASK THE RIGHT QUESTIONS

None of this means that lawyers must learn to build neural networks or develop their own agentic workflows. The role of the lawyer remains fundamentally the same: advise clients (whether external or internal), interpret the law, and help solve complex problems.

But the tools used to deliver that advice are evolving quickly, and lawyers who understand the fundamentals of AI will be better equipped to select appropriate use cases, supervise outputs, and identify new opportunities for improving legal services.

The goal of this chapter has not been to make lawyers into technologists. It has been to ensure that when a lawyer sits across from a vendor, reviews an AI output, or decides which task to trust to a tool, they know what questions to ask.

THE LAWYER'S MENTAL MODEL OF AI

In a Sentence

Lawyers do not need to become technical experts in AI but in order to use it effectively and safely they do need a working understanding of how it functions, and they need to know its strengths and limitations.

Six concepts worth remembering

- » *Tokens and context windows.* AI reads text in small units called tokens. The context window is the working memory that holds both the input and the response. During extended use, older content can fall out of that window and be, in effect, forgotten.
- » *Hallucinations.* Generative AI is designed to *sound* correct, not to *be* correct. It predicts likely text and has no built-in mechanism for checking whether what it produces is true.
- » *Attention and transformers.* The transformer allows whole passages and documents to be read at once, weighing how each word relates to every other word.
- » *Retrieval-augmented generation.* RAG is how a model accesses information it was not trained on, such as documents from a specific matter file. RAG is the right tool for searching across databases where the relevant material is not known in advance, but it can be skipped if you already know the documents that matter.

- *The five functional categories*: predictive (forecasting outcomes), classification (sorting content), extraction (pulling named facts), generative (drafting new text), and reasoning (stepping through a problem before answering). A single legal AI platform often combines several.
- *Agents and Model Context Protocol.* Agents move AI beyond a chatbot into a true digital colleague, able to carry out multi-step work across different systems. MCP is the plumbing that lets agents reach those systems in a structured way.

One question to leave with

- The next time you sit across from a vendor, a client, a regulator, or an anxious partner, ask yourself whether you have enough of this language to ask the right questions or whether there is a concept above that you would find hard to explain.

CHAPTER 3

Strategic Considerations: Pricing, Revenue, and the Future of the Law Firm–Client Relationship

Now that we are acquainted with why AI matters to law and how it might affect the work that lawyers do, this chapter turns to more fundamental questions. How does AI impact the underlying strategy of a law firm or a legal team? What major decisions does AI force leadership to make?

If AI were simply a better tool than those that were previously available, the strategic implications for legal teams would be modest. Firms would buy software, train lawyers, and move on. In-house teams would rely on their organizations to use the latest technology when delivering legal services. But AI is not simply a better tool. It possesses a general-purpose capability that will inevitably reshape how work is priced; how value is articulated; how, and how many, people are recruited into law firms and in-house legal departments; how their time and work are rewarded; and the ways in which firms decide which markets they can profitably serve.

Importantly, when we discuss the strategic considerations of AI, we are *not* referring to an AI strategy. Or, at least, we are not talking about an AI strategy that sits separately from the wider firm strategy. There are, of course, necessary considerations about procurement, deployment, effective adoption mechanisms, and measurement, for example, that may sit within a plan, but the cascading effects of AI have to be embedded in the overall direction of the organization. It would be impossible to consider changes to pricing, talent, workflows, and the types of work that will be delivered using AI without factoring them into the broader direction of the business. How to use AI is not a technology decision but a commercial one, as it is a development that is likely to have the most impact on the previously unshakeable billable hour – one way or another.

Although firms and legal teams are experimenting enthusiastically with AI tools, far fewer are confronting the strategic consequences of what those tools make possible. AI does not solely accelerate existing work, it also makes some work cheaper and some work possible that was not previously viable at all. Each of those outcomes has a strategic implication, and those implications do not all point in the same direction. They destabilize long-standing assumptions about pricing, leverage, value, and, crucially, what law firms are actually selling to their clients and what in-house teams deploy within their teams.

FROM TIME TO OUTCOMES: PRICING IN AN AI-ENABLED WORLD

Pricing for Value

As discussed in chapter 1, few topics generate as much anxiety in law practice as pricing does. As we have seen, the billable hour has survived not because it is elegant, but because it is administratively simple. It provides a common unit of measurement across practice areas, jurisdictions, and seniority levels. For decades it has been the default proxy for value.

Alternative fee arrangements (AFAs) – that is, any arrangement that is not the standard billable hour – are not new. Fixed fees, capped fees, and contingency fees have existed for a long time. Recent years have also seen the rise of effective fee arrangements (EFAs). Under an EFA, a firm bases its pricing on the value of the output of the provision of legal services instead of the time it took. This allows law firms and their clients to find a happy compromise over fees that reflects the expertise required to deliver the solution that meets the client's needs without the disincentive to efficiency that the billable hour creates.

Finishing matters faster is also not just a case of cost saving. For in-house teams it represents the freedom to move forward more quickly with whatever legal matter is in play, whether that is settling a legal dispute so that work may continue, completing a transaction, or closing sooner so that business as usual can proceed. Put simply, time has reversed value for the client. The faster you deliver, the more value you create, particularly for publicly traded companies where market timing is critical and management attention is finite. The longer a transaction drags on, the harder it becomes for the business to operate normally.

Historically, many AFAs have been adopted defensively. Although AFAs and EFAs are not new concepts in the legal profession, they are more prevalent in transactional practices in Europe and Asia. This is not because firms embraced outcome-based pricing of their own accord but because clients demanded cost certainty and firms absorbed the risk through write-downs and write-offs to remain competitive. In the United States, however, especially in the BigLaw market, outcome-based pricing is not yet the norm. What *is* new is the way AI changes the economic logic underlying fee considerations for clients globally, and the ability to measure and predict service costs in advance.

AI changes that risk profile from defensive to tactical. Tasks that were once unpredictable in delivery become more consistent. The uncertainty introduced by a variable volume of documents or manual processes begins to fade. First-pass document reviews, selective reviews, and issue spotting can now be carried out with greater consistency, particularly in high-volume contexts such as due diligence and eDiscovery. This has happened more rapidly in jurisdictions where due diligence is a distinct, scoped exercise. In the United States, where deal size and liability concerns differ, the same approach has been slower to take hold. The size of the deal still matters for pricing purposes, but certainty now counts more. Even there, however, the conversation has shifted from *whether* AI can be used to *where* it should be used and *how much certainty* it provides.

Some clients have pushed their counsel further still. The authors have been informed of a number of UK-based institutional clients that have begun experimenting with credit-based fee structures that tie payment directly to innovation and knowledge-sharing. Roughly speaking, this model sees fees being paid up to a negotiated cap, after which the firm enters a credit zone. Fees accrued in that zone are only payable if the firm has delivered agreed extras over the course of the year, whether that is an innovation project, a secondment, or a knowledge-sharing initiative. If the firm has not delivered on those commitments, the client is entitled to withhold payment entirely for the overage.

Whether this model spreads widely or remains confined to a handful of sophisticated buyers is yet to be seen. What matters is the underlying premise that clients in certain jurisdictions are no longer simply negotiating rates downwards; instead they are redesigning the structure of the engagement itself and embedding expectations about technology, innovation, and value directly into the commercial terms. The fee arrangement is being asked to do more than account for hours worked. As noted, in the United States, where the willingness to pay for time remains more entrenched, particularly in large-scale transactions, this kind of restructuring has not yet taken hold. But for firms operating across jurisdictions, the divergence should be instructive, if not a harbinger. What looks like a jurisdiction-specific development may well be an early signal of where the broader market is headed.

Clients were never buying time. That is not why they engage their panel law firms. What clients are buying is confidence. They are buying expertise. They are paying for the firm's judgement about where risk lies, how reviews should be structured, and what *not* to look at. And, if we are being fully honest, they are paying for the security of the law firm's insurance should things go awry. If we concede that clients buy confidence, then charging for outcomes makes much more sense. Charging for results rather than time forces firms to articulate what 'value' actually means. Cost savings alone are rarely the full story, and the benefits of faster deals – such as accelerating time to market, freeing up management attention, and fast-tracking commercial decisions – still accrue even if the overall fee broadly remains the same. The strategic question for firms is whether they are prepared to price for that value explicitly.

Case Study: Scaling Due Diligence Through AI

At one international firm, the Corporate M&A team needed a way to increase the value of the due diligence exercise for clients while increasing efficiency in extracting information from datarooms. In partnership with a leading legal AI tool, the team developed a solution that used a templated review table to automatically extract information from dataroom documents so that it could be reviewed by the lawyers. Not only did this make due diligence more efficient, but it also meant that clients could benefit from a review of more documents, not having to rely on review of only the most material documents as may have been the case in the past.

AI-Enhanced Pricing

Although pricing methods vary from one law firm to the next, part of the reason firms are unwilling to shift away from the billable hour is that it is tried-and-true and has worked for years. As

Richard Susskind has said: 'It's hard to convince a room full of millionaires that they've got their business model wrong.'[1] While some teams use technology to support pricing decisions, AI and its ability to parse large sets of data in natural language provides the potential to divide up the essential elements of a matter like never before. Matter codes, hours, and narratives can be uploaded to present options for average prices for phases, and these charges can be reviewed against the proportions of written-down (before the bill goes out) or written-off (after the bill is received by the client) time from law firms to better identify the 'value' of any phase of a matter.

As clients become more sophisticated in how they evaluate legal spend, firms that can demonstrate data-driven pricing will have a meaningful competitive advantage in winning and retaining work. A firm that can show a client, with specificity, how a proposed fee was calculated, what the historical range has been for comparable matters, and where the firm expects to deliver efficiency gains is having a fundamentally different conversation than a firm that quotes a rate and hopes the client does not push back. This is also, critically, another argument for the data strategy we will discuss in chapter 5.

Clean, structured matter data is not an abstract good. It is the foundation on which defensible pricing rests. A firm that cannot pull accurate historical data on how long a phase of work typically takes, how much of that time was written down, and what the effective realization rate was for similar matters is flying blind when it quotes a fee. AI can surface these patterns, but only if the underlying data is reliable. Firms with messy billing narratives, inconsistent matter coding, and fragmented time records will find that their AI-generated pricing models are only as good as what they are built on. The firms that have invested in data hygiene will be able to price with confidence, to justify those prices to increasingly sceptical clients, and to adapt their fee structures as the market demands. Those that have not will continue to price by instinct and hope that both instinct and the collections hold.

Beyond pricing, those same tools also allow law firms to answer the 'What's market?' question with precision across various situations. For example, how is a certain provision most commonly worded? What legal or business terms are standard? They also help a law firm to market its expertise, find internal experts, and optimize work allocation.

Charging for Knowledge, Not Technology

One of the most striking shifts in recent conversations has been the way clients talk about what they are *not* willing to pay for. There is growing resistance to the idea of being charged for 'technology', particularly where that technology feels generic. At the same time, there is a clear willingness to pay for embedded expertise.

This distinction has precedent. In eDiscovery, clients historically paid third-party vendors directly. When law firms brought eDiscovery in-house, clients continued to pay, albeit sometimes at a reduced rate, because the service remained visible and familiar. Due diligence, by contrast, never carried a separate hosting or infrastructure cost. Clients were not used to paying for the mechanics of review, only for the lawyers' output.

AI brings this tension into sharp relief. Firms that attempt to charge explicitly for tools often struggle, especially as more and more in-house teams procure the same technology. Firms that frame their offering as access to institutional knowledge, professional judgement, and insurance coverage find the conversation easier. Value billing in this sense becomes about providing an answer backed by professional confidence and accountability. In one recent example, a client developed a bespoke tool for withholding tax review and asked all of its panel firms to use it as part of the transaction workflow. The tool generated outputs and the client knew the outputs were good. And yet the instruction to the firms was that they still needed to check it because their insurance was needed as cover.

This gets to the heart of where the value proposition of law firms may ultimately settle. The client was not primarily concerned with the analysis; they had already done that themselves. They were more concerned with the professional accountability that sits behind the analysis, and with the ability, if something goes wrong, to look to the firm and its professional indemnity cover rather than to an internally built tool and the people who built it. Even in a world where clients are technically capable of doing more of the work themselves, the demand for external legal assurance might not diminish. It might simply change shape.

This also explains the growing interest in subscription models, bespoke builds, and modular offerings. Some elements of a firm's knowledge can be packaged and reused. Others are inherently client specific, drawing on prior matters, playbooks, and accumulated experience. The strategic challenge is in deciding what should be general, what should remain bespoke, and how far a firm is prepared to let that knowledge travel outside the firm.

Advising Clients on AI as a Distinct Service Line

Even as some, or even many, rote tasks get swept in-house, more clients might turn to their counsel for advice on how to deploy AI within their own legal operations. The logic is understandable. Law firms – or at least those firms that have invested seriously in AI adoption – have spent the last two years navigating procurement, data governance, change management, and risk. These are precisely the issues that in-house teams are now confronting for the first time.

This creates two distinct but related revenue opportunities. The first is product related: giving clients access to a tool or workflow the firm has built, often on a subscription or licensing basis. The second is advisory: helping the client think through its own AI strategy, evaluate vendors, and make decisions about where and how to deploy technology. The two are connected, but they require different capabilities, different pricing, and different conversations.

A firm that conflates these opportunities risks undervaluing both. And a firm that ignores the advisory opportunity altogether might find that the clients who once relied on it for legal judgement are now also looking elsewhere for strategic guidance on technology. This is a conversation that, if lost, might never come back.

Case Study: Macfarlanes AI Policy Service

When rolling out AI across their organizations, in-house legal teams are increasingly looking to law firms to assess the practical and strategic implications of implementation. In 2025 Macfarlanes launched a new multidisciplinary initiative providing clients with advice on AI policy that covered legal and regulatory advice, along with technological advice such as potential issues around the capabilities of the technology, server locations, and practical considerations during deployment and use. This approach utilizes the skills of specialist lawyers and technologists in collaboration to deliver a holistic service.

INNOVATION AS A ROUTE TO NEW MARKETS

Partnering with AI

Much of the early AI narrative in law has focused on cost reduction. While efficiency clearly matters, particularly in a market under sustained fee pressure, it is rarely transformative on its own in the long run. The more strategically interesting question relates to what new markets become accessible when delivery costs fall.

Not only does AI reduce cost, it also opens up markets that were previously uneconomic. Several firms are already using AI-enabled workflows to move down-market, taking on smaller matters at scale and profiting from doing so. The logic is straightforward: if the marginal cost of delivery falls, the addressable market expands.

This is where we encounter a fork in the road between evolution and revolution. The *evolutionary* approach looks at AI through the lens of the existing business: doing the same work faster, charging less to win more, and reducing non-billable downtime between matters. All of that is valuable, but it is also 'looking under the streetlight'. The *revolutionary* lens asks, 'What entirely new capability does AI create?' That is, what work that was never previously viable, in markets that were never previously addressable, is now possible? The firms that thrive will be those that can straddle the two approaches.

Some of the firms that are moving fastest are doing so not by building alone, but by partnering with vendors to co-develop. A certain subset of those firms is then making those co-developed products or modules available down-market to their peer firms. This raises some difficult questions about proprietary advantage: for example, how much of a firm's 'secret sauce' can be codified without eroding differentiation? In practice the answer often lies in what the workflow is pointed at. Generic modules may be widely usable, but the real value emerges when they are combined with client-specific data, prior deal history, and contextual judgement. In other words, it is likely to be less about the workflow itself and more about the knowledge that fuels it.

There is a strategic opportunity here for firms with uneven coverage. A strong central workflow library from a vendor can allow a firm to support smaller or emerging practice areas, where the technology acts as a thought partner if a deep lawyer bench strength does not yet exist.

Market Disruption

There is a further dimension to these partnerships that firms would do well to consider carefully. When a firm co-develops a workflow with a client or a vendor, the knowledge flows in both directions. The firm gains a capability tailored to its practice and the vendor gains something arguably more valuable: deep insight into how lawyers actually work. Every workflow co-developed with a firm teaches the vendor what matters in that practice area, what the decision points are, how experienced lawyers think through problems, and what good looks like. That knowledge does not stay locked inside the partnership.

It may inform the vendor's product roadmap, its generic offerings, and ultimately the tools it sells to every other firm in the market. Firms that choose to co-develop and keep the resulting workflows proprietary may preserve a temporary advantage, but they should be clear-eyed about the fact that the underlying intelligence has already been absorbed. Firms that co-develop and publicize their work make a different bet: that the reputational and market-positioning benefits of being seen as a leader outweigh the risk of competitors learning from the example. Both strategies are defensible. What is not defensible is co-developing with the belief that the knowledge shared with a vendor remains exclusively yours. Legal-technology vendors, by the nature of their work, aggregate institutional intelligence from dozens of the world's most sophisticated law firms. The firms building with them are not just buying a product; they are also contributing to one.

THE BILLABLE HOUR, REVISITED

Predictions about the death of the billable hour are not new, and we will not rehash them again here. What is worth saying is why that model has proved so durable. Hours remain the most practical way to understand the economics of a matter, because real estate, technology, and talent are largely sunk costs and time is the one variable a firm controls. And for all but the most commoditized work, it is genuinely difficult to know whether a given fixed fee is the right number. Clients do not want to overpay, firms need a cushion against scope creep, and the two sides often cannot agree on a fixed fee at all. The billable hour survives not because anyone loves it, but because it sidesteps a pricing problem that neither party has been able to solve. What AI disrupts is not the existence of the hour but its dominance as the sole measure of value.

The evidence increasingly suggests that firms that invest now in understanding how AI changes their work, their pricing, and their client relationships will compound that knowledge over time. Those who wait until the pressure becomes unavoidable will find themselves trying to build in a year what their competitors built over five.

REVENUE, REDUCTION, AND OPPORTUNITY COST

A recurring mistake when it comes to AI strategy is treating it purely as a cost-reduction exercise. Efficiency matters, but efficiency alone does not create an advantage. What matters is what you do with the capacity you free up.

If AI allows work to be completed faster, firms face a choice. They can charge less and win more work, reducing non-billable time between matters, or they can redeploy that capacity into higher-value advisory work, product development, or new markets. Either way, the relevant metric is opportunity cost, not hours saved.

Assessing this requires firms to be honest about profitability by practice area. Some practices are highly exposed to automation; others are less so. A litigation-support function that relies on high volumes of junior review time faces a very different calculus from a regulatory advisory practice built on senior judgement. Data can be used to rank where investment in AI will have the greatest strategic impact, taking into account not only margin but also future risk. A practice that is profitable today but structurally vulnerable to automation in three to five years needs attention now, not when the revenue starts to decline.

Preparing for extreme futures, even those that seem unlikely, is often the best way to remain resilient whatever happens. A firm that invests in data hygiene, workflow automation, and flexible pricing structures because it believes disruption is imminent will find itself better positioned even if disruption proves gradual. The converse – a firm that assumes continuity and invests accordingly – is far more vulnerable if that assumption turns out to be wrong. The range of plausible futures for the legal profession is wider than it has been in living memory, and that uncertainty alone is a reason to act.

FROM ASSESSMENT TO ACTION: A FRAMEWORK FOR STRATEGIC PRIORITIZATION

Knowing that opportunity cost matters is one thing, but knowing where to start is another. Not every practice area will be equally affected, and not every investment will yield the same return. The challenge is to develop a structured way of deciding where to focus, one that accounts for both the urgency of the disruption and the commercial importance of the work at risk.

Some firms have begun to develop structured frameworks for exactly this kind of analysis, with the approach typically involving two overlapping assessments.

The first occurs at the practice level and includes interviewing partners and senior associates and examining data to understand, in concrete terms, what percentage of the work within each practice area is susceptible to automation and how quickly that change is likely to arrive. What do associates spend their first two years doing? How much of that is pattern based? How much requires genuine judgement? The answers to these questions produce a measure of exposure grounded in the experience of the people doing the work, not in vendor marketing materials.

The second assessment is commercial and involves ranking each practice area by profitability, revenue contribution, and strategic importance to the firm. A small practice group generating modest revenue may not warrant significant AI investment, regardless of how exposed it is. A core profit driver facing even moderate disruption demands immediate attention.

The value of combining these two assessments is that it forces a conversation the partnership might otherwise avoid. If a practice area is both highly exposed and highly profitable, the firm cannot afford to wait. If it is exposed but marginal, the conversation is different. And if it is profitable but not yet exposed, the questions are whether that will remain true and, if the answer to the first question is uncertain, what preparation should look like. Is there a 50% chance that this work looks fundamentally different in three years? If so, what would we do about it? And if the probability is only 10%, does the severity of the outcome still justify preparing?

Rather than producing a single answer, the framework produces a prioritized set of questions, and that is often more useful than a prescriptive plan in a landscape that is changing this quickly.

WHY THERE CANNOT BE A STANDALONE AI STRATEGY, REVISITED

We opened this chapter by arguing that an AI strategy cannot exist in a vacuum. It is worth returning to that point, because the practical implications are hopefully clearer now.

Clients are beginning to ask two very specific questions. How much money will you save me by doing this task with AI? And what is the delta between how long this work took you manually and how long it takes you with AI? Rather than being abstractions, these are the beginning of an A/B testing exercise that, once completed at scale, will produce data with profound consequences for how firms are structured, how they hire, and potentially how the partnership model itself operates.

Consider what happens when a firm can answer those questions with precision. The data will show that some categories of work are susceptible to the Jevons paradox (see chapter 8 for additional discussion).[2] AI makes the work faster, which means there is more work because clients who previously could not justify the cost now can. Contract review that once took forty hours and cost accordingly might now take four, making it viable for smaller deals, more frequent reviews, and broader coverage. The total volume of work may increase even as the per-unit cost falls. Other categories of work may go in the opposite direction entirely. Due diligence, for instance, may become so automated that it ceases to be chargeable as a standalone service. Instead it becomes a cost of doing business, built into the fee for the transaction rather than billed separately, or it becomes something the in-house team does itself for certain transactions. And still other categories will shift because clients, equipped with the same AI tools as their law firms, bring more and more of the routine work in-house. What they come to the firm for, as we have noted, is the knowledge, the judgement, and the insurance that AI cannot provide on its own.

Each of these outcomes points the business in a different direction. One suggests hiring more people to handle greater volume at lower margins. Another suggests hiring fewer people and charging differently. A third suggests restructuring the firm's offering around expertise instead of process. No firm will face only one of these futures, and most will face all three simultaneously, across different practice areas, different client segments, and different jurisdictions. And that is precisely why an AI strategy cannot stand apart from a firm's overall strategy. The technology has reached a point where it does not merely support the business, it informs the direction the business is about to take.

How a firm hires, how it structures its teams, how it prices, how it decides what work to pursue and what work to walk away from – all of these decisions are now entangled with the capabilities that AI provides. A firm that treats AI as a technology initiative managed by the innovation team, separate from the conversations happening in the boardroom about growth, hiring, and market positioning, will find that the two strategies diverge until one of them becomes irrelevant. They must grow in parallel, because in practice they are no longer two strategies at all. They are the same strategy seen from different angles.

WHAT DISTINGUISHES THE LEADERS

The firms that will pull ahead in the short to medium term share a recognizable set of characteristics that are already visible across the various threads discussed so far.

Firstly, the firms that will succeed are those that are willing to cannibalize current revenue in exchange for future positioning. They accept that some categories of work will generate less income as AI makes them faster and cheaper, and they do not try to protect those margins artificially. Instead, they redeploy the capacity into higher-value advisory work, new service lines, or deeper client relationships. They treat the short-term reduction in revenue per matter as an investment, not a loss.

Secondly, they invest in knowledge infrastructure before they invest in tools. They understand that the quality of AI output depends entirely on the quality of the data and on the institutional knowledge behind that data, and they have committed real resources to cleaning, structuring, and governing it. They have hired or developed people whose job is specifically to make the firm's accumulated knowledge accessible to AI systems, recognizing that this requires different skills and different thinking than traditional knowledge management.

Thirdly, those firms embed AI into core workflows rather than running it as a side experiment. Instead of confining the technology to an innovation lab or a pilot programme, it becomes part of how work gets done on live matters, with real clients, under real time pressure. The difference between a pilot and an embedded workflow is the difference between knowing that AI works in theory and knowing how it performs under the conditions that actually matter.

And fourthly, the firms that are most likely to thrive align incentives with the behaviours they want to see. If adoption is a strategic priority, then it should be reflected in how people are evaluated, how they are compensated, and how their contribution is recognized. Firms that tell lawyers to use AI while continuing to reward them exclusively for billable hours are sending a contradictory message that lawyers are smart enough to read. The firms that are leading have found ways, whether through contribution hours, adoption bonuses, or explicit recognition in the promotion process, to make the new behaviours professionally rational.

None of this is easy, and none of it produces overnight results. But the gap between firms that are doing these things and firms that are still deliberating is already widening, and it will only compound.

TOOLS WITHOUT TRANSFORMATION

One final point before we close this chapter. Tools are meaningless without the cultural and organizational conditions that allow them to be used well. A firm can invest in the most sophisticated AI platform on the market, price it into its fee arrangements, and build workflows around it, but they could still fail to realize the strategic value if the people expected to use it are not equipped, incentivized, or culturally permitted to do so. Rather than being a *technology* problem, the gap between procurement and adoption is a *human* problem, and it is where many of the strategic ambitions discussed in this chapter will ultimately succeed or fail. The chapters that follow will examine this in detail: the skills required, the training that works, the governance that enables rather than restricts, and the change management that turns a software procurement into a genuine shift in how a firm operates.

IN PRACTICE

In a Sentence

The decisions that AI forces on an organization or practice are business decisions: what you are selling, how work gets done, how you price it or show the value derived from it, which parts of today's revenue you are prepared to walk away from, and where new sources of revenue might originate.

What to Remember

» Clients were never buying time. They are buying confidence, expertise, and the security of the firm's insurance.

» Value-based pricing is philosophically attractive but tactically risky. AI has shifted enough of that risk for it to become a live option.

» There is no standalone AI strategy. AI use and aspirations have to align with, and be embedded into, the firm's overarching strategy.

» Data hygiene comes before pricing discipline. If you cannot see how you have handled and priced historically for phases of work, you are flying blind when quoting fees.

» Leaders distinguish themselves through a willingness to think long term about the business model instead of yearly revenue. Adopting AI is not, on its own, what sets an organization apart.

What to Do with This

» Rank each practice by automation exposure (from partner or team-lead interviews) and by commercial weight (profitability, strategic importance). Invest where both scores are high. Attend to that quadrant before its revenue starts to fall.

- » Protect time and budget for experimentation that is not expected to be billable.
- » Align incentives with the behaviour you want. Credit AI use against hours targets, or build an innovation component into bonus and promotion criteria. Do not ask people to optimize in opposition to the billable hour while rewarding them only for maximizing time spent.
- » For each major matter type, talk to your clients and decide whether you will price by outcome, fixed fee, capped fee, or hourly. Explain your reasoning because that is as important as the answer itself.

Questions to Sit With

- » Will the work in your most profitable practice look fundamentally different in three years? If so, what should you do about it today?
- » If your largest client asked tomorrow for the 'delta' (what the work used to cost before AI, compared with what it should cost now), could you answer?
- » Which of your services, if you do not cannibalize them yourself, will a competitor or client cannibalize for you? What differentiates you?

CHAPTER 4

Building a Team

THE RIGHT TEAM WITH THE RIGHT SKILLS

Chapters 1 and 2 set out what AI is, why it matters to the legal profession, and why lawyers should care about its impacts. Chapter 3 explored the (potentially existential) strategic consequences of this technology. This chapter turns to the people who can and do make it all work, specifically the teams, roles, structures, and skills required to move from experimentation to execution.

AI does not deploy itself. Nor does it organize itself neatly into the existing structures of a law firm or corporate legal department. The implications of this technology cut across the business in ways that few previous technologies have. The question of where AI 'lives' within an organization is not merely administrative, it determines who selects tools, who supports them, who trains lawyers to use them, and who ensures they are deployed and used responsibly. Get the structure wrong and the result is duplication, political friction, and shadow AI. Get it right and the organization can move faster, more coherently, and with greater confidence.

This chapter addresses three interrelated questions. First, where should AI capability sit within a business? Second, what roles are needed to support it? And third, what skills do the wider organization and its lawyers need to develop to use it well?

So what does good actually look like? AI capability belongs close enough to the work that the people building it understand what lawyers do all day, and close enough to leadership that it can shape strategy rather than just service requests. The roles that support it include a mix of lawyers who have learned the technology and technologists who have learned the law, working together instead of handing things back and forth. None of this happens on its own; it happens because a firm decides that it should, and will, build the structures necessary to make it real.

WHERE DOES AI LIVE?

Does AI Live with IT?

AI touches knowledge management, innovation, IT infrastructure, libraries and information services, risk and compliance, and every practice group. The danger is that when something belongs to everyone, it often ends up belonging to no one.

There is a strong consensus, borne out across firms of all sizes and geographies, that AI capability should not sit primarily within IT. While IT plays an essential role in infrastructure, security, and integration, the deployment of AI tools in a legal context requires a nuanced understanding of the practice of law that is not a core IT competency. Some firms have placed AI within IT departments, and in certain configurations this can work, but in most cases it calls for a closer relationship with the lawyers and the work they do.

Of course, all AI tools that come into a firm should align with the security standards, policies, infrastructure, and interoperability requirements the IT vertical has determined are required for any technology solution. However, when it comes to developing end-user deployment initiatives, engagement and adoption frameworks, and training mechanisms, firms are best served by investing in people who have experience not just in the technology but also in the law.

There is a further reason why AI and AI leadership should sit outside IT. Adopting AI affects the business model of the organization, fundamentally reshaping how people work. Leading that change is less a technical challenge than a persuasive one. It requires both the telling of stories about what is possible and the building of enough trust that lawyers are willing to change the way they work. That is a different skill set from infrastructure management, and it benefits from sitting closer to the practice.

Does AI Live with Knowledge or Innovation? One Department, One Voice

A recurring lesson is that knowledge management and innovation should sit within the same vertical. Where they are separated, they tend to develop competing agendas. While they both focus on 'making lawyers practise smarter', they come from different perspectives. Knowledge teams focus on substantive legal content and training; their goal is to keep the lawyers in their practice up to date on developments in the law and to manage their precedent documents effectively. Innovation teams focus on improved processes and technology, and how advances in technology can help lawyers do their work more effectively. But innovators may be generalists, often without a thorough understanding of every practice group. Over time, these agendas may diverge and create friction, both internally and in the way each group engages with the practice.

AI has amplified this friction because it sits squarely in both camps. It is simultaneously a knowledge tool (it drafts, it researches, it structures precedent) and an innovation tool (it automates, it reimagines processes, it changes how work is delivered). If the two functions are separate, they will both claim ownership and neither will deploy it coherently.

The authors have been informed of one instance where a firm learned this the hard way. When building out its knowledge and innovation function, leadership allocated a budget for two directors (one for knowledge, one for innovation). A senior candidate refused the split. She would only take the role if she could lead both. Leadership overruled her and hired for the roles separately, and within months the two directors were pulling in different directions, creating exactly the kind of fragmentation a combined role is meant to prevent. With the benefit of hindsight, it is clear that the candidate was right to push back against the split. When knowledge and innovation report to different leaders, the result is two agendas competing for the same attention, and neither gets enough of it.

The skills required for knowledge and innovation functions are genuinely unique. Pure knowledge management professionals bring deep legal expertise, familiarity with precedent, and the ability to structure and maintain institutional knowledge. Innovation professionals bring change management capability; technology fluency; and the ability to assess, pilot, and deploy new tools. These are rarely the same person. Finding a single candidate who has the right combination of skills is like finding a unicorn. But the two skill sets must be coordinated, and the most effective way to do that is to house them under a single leadership structure, even if they operate as distinct teams within the department.

Historically, innovation teams have taken the lead on legal technology training, using concrete practice-specific examples to demonstrate a tool's potential, while knowledge lawyers contextualize those capabilities for day-to-day legal work. The most effective model appears to be one where the knowledge lawyer acts as the front-facing ambassador to the practice, empowered and supported by innovation and legal technology professionals who work behind the scenes on tool configuration, training scripts, and deployment. This approach maintains trust with the lawyers, who see a familiar face with credible legal knowledge (the knowledge manager) who is backed by technology that is being monitored and deployed effectively (by the innovation team).

There is a shift happening here, too. Knowledge lawyers who once focused exclusively on substantive training are beginning to recognize that the technology helps them do their job better, and they are therefore shifting towards an interest in involvement in the end-to-end process of technology evaluation and deployment. That realization, when it arrives, is the moment the two functions stop competing and start reinforcing each other.

Centralization and Practice Alignment

One of the more contentious structural questions is whether knowledge lawyers should report centrally or directly to the partners in the practice groups they support. In many firms, knowledge lawyers are embedded within practices and report to practice heads. While this creates strong relationships with the lawyers they serve, it often results in fragmentation. Without central coordination, each practice develops its own solutions, selects its own tools, and operates without the benefit of shared best practices across the firm.

The recommended approach, borne out by several firms that have tested both models, is centralization but with strong practice affiliation. Knowledge and innovation professionals report to a central chief or director but are allocated to, and maintain close relationships with, specific practices. This structure preserves the subject-matter alignment that makes knowledge professionals effective while ensuring firm-wide consistency in tool selection, deployment standards, and strategic direction.

The worst outcome, and one that is more common than firms care to admit, is where the organization chart says one thing and reality says another. Knowledge lawyers may technically report to a central function, but in practice they take direction exclusively from the partners in the practice they specialize in. This creates accountability gaps and inconsistent adoption, and it makes firm-wide strategic initiatives nearly impossible to execute – not to mention the fact that it creates feelings of rudderlessness among the knowledge lawyers. A knowledge lawyer who feels, rightly or wrongly, that their real boss is the practice head rather than the central director will prioritize accordingly. And in a partnership, where the partners are the owners of the business, that gravitational pull is difficult to resist. The structure has to be real, not merely aspirational. Central reporting must come with actual authority over priorities, tool selection, and deployment standards, otherwise it is just an organizational chart that nobody follows.

The AI Committee

An AI Committee is not optional. It is the mechanism through which competing priorities are managed, initiatives are selected, and scarce resources are allocated. The AI Committee also serves a purpose that goes well beyond technology decisions. As adoption scales and usage data accumulate, the committee becomes the body with the clearest picture of how AI is actually changing the work across the firm: which practices are seeing real efficiency gains; where headcount assumptions are starting to shift; and what clients are asking for or pushing back on. The strategic questions we explored in chapter 3 – about pricing, hiring, leverage, and how the partnership model itself may need to evolve – cannot be answered from the boardroom alone. They require the kind of granular, practice-level intelligence that only comes from watching AI reshape workflows in real time. If constituted correctly and provided with the right data, this is what the AI Committee will see, and it is why firm leadership will increasingly come to this body not just for technology recommendations, but for the data that informs the firm's most consequential decisions about its future direction.

The committee should be heavily driven by lawyers. Business services – including representatives from IT, knowledge, innovation, business development, general counsel, and risk – should attend and be represented, but the committee's legitimacy depends on it being recognized as a body that speaks for the firm's practice and not just its support functions. Its core job is to prioritize. There are two fundamental scarcities in rolling out and testing AI technology: first, lawyer time and attention; and second, IT capacity to support integration and back-end deployment. Because both are finite, decisions have to be taken. The committee is where those choices are made, transparently, with input from the people most affected.

The committee's second most important role is to help with change management and adoption channels. Having practising lawyers on the committee both gives the committee legitimacy and helps immeasurably when they act as ambassadors to win hearts and minds.

The ideal size is modest: no more than a dozen regular members. All that is needed is a handful of partners and a handful of business services representatives, with the ability to invite guests as specific topics require. Representation from multiple practice areas is essential.

There is a question of scope. Some firms separate the committee into two bodies or subgroups: one focused on governance, risk, policy, and financial implications; and another focused on engagement, adoption, and rollout. Others combine both within a single body. There is no single correct answer, but the preference of most firms that have tried both is that a single body with subgroups is preferable to entirely separate structures. Policies that are developed without practitioner input risk being ignored or, worse, creating the conditions for shadow AI by being too restrictive to follow in practice. If associates feel that the firm's AI policy was written in a vacuum by people who do not use the tools, they will work around it. They will go to ChatGPT or Claude on their personal accounts and do the work there, outside the firm's governance framework entirely. Done right, the AI policy should not scare lawyers away but should instead serve as a tool to drive adoption by providing clarity and setting expectations.

The general counsel or risk function should have a meaningful role in the committee, with the authority to sign off on what can and cannot be deployed. This additionally serves the practical purpose of having a risk voice in the room to provide institutional authority when mandatory training or compliance requirements need to be enforced.

The committee also provides a mechanism for saying no. In a partnership, where political capital is finite and individual partners are accustomed to getting what they want, declining an initiative is difficult without backing. With a trusted, representative body, however, decisions to deprioritize or decline carry more weight and are harder to circumvent. A prioritization matrix, signed off by the committee and reviewed quarterly, ensures that the firm is allocating its limited resources strategically rather than chasing the latest technology because everyone else appears to be doing so.

Where Does AI Live in In-House Teams and Smaller Firms

The same principles apply to in-house legal departments and smaller firms, even if the structures are more compressed. The scale is different but the logic is the same. In-house teams should invite practitioners to participate and create champions who will advocate for adoption within their own areas. These champions are also essential when the time comes for change management. Rolling out a tool without input from the lawyers who will use it invites the same resistance in-house as it does in a law firm. If lawyers have not been heard and have not been given a chance to influence the process, they are far more likely to reject what is presented to them.

In-house legal teams should also ensure they are represented on any business-wide AI Committee. Legal is not always given a seat at the table in enterprise-level AI discussions, but the regulatory, ethical, and operational implications of AI make legal representation essential. The alternative is that decisions about tools, data, and risk are made without legal input, and legal is left to manage the consequences after the fact.

Smaller firms face a different version of the same problem. In a firm of 300 lawyers, the entire AI Committee might effectively be one person, namely, the chief innovation officer, meeting informally with practice heads and directors. That can work, particularly when the firm is small enough that everyone can sit around a single table. But even in that context, the discipline of including practitioner voices and of having partners and associates involved in decisions about what to prioritize makes a material difference to the quality of the decisions and the likelihood of adoption. A decision that comes from the innovation team alone is a recommendation. A decision that comes from a body that includes the practice is a mandate.

A Home for AI

As mentioned at the start of this chapter, it might seem like AI lives everywhere in an organization. Almost every technology tool a firm onboards now either includes or is intending to include AI capabilities. But the structure best positioned to drive cohesive deployment is a combined innovation and knowledge team, close to the practice and close to leadership, supported by an AI Committee composed of partners and business specialists providing the authority and strategic direction. IT underpins the structure. It owns the security standards, manages the integrations, maintains the infrastructure on which every AI tool depends, and ensures that what gets deployed meets the firm's technical and compliance requirements.

Within that combined team, mature departments are increasingly splitting work into distinct subfunctions. They might be called different things, but the core functions are generally as follows.

- A knowledge management and innovation team acts as the face of the department to the practice, owning precedents, expertise location, and the process redesign that makes practice groups AI-ready.

- A data science and legal engineering team builds the firm's own AI solutions, including the agents and models, and the analytics dashboards that sit on top of them.
- A practice solutions team, typically led by product managers, owns vendor relationships (see chapter 10) and maintains the user experience layer for the tools the firm has licensed.
- A dedicated engagement and transformation function owns the change management work that turns deployment into adoption, including internal and external communication, listening sessions and feedback collection, the AI narrative the firm takes to clients, and the measurement of adoption itself.

Smaller firms will inevitably combine these, but the underlying principle that these are different jobs requiring different skills holds at any size.

AI-ENABLING ROLES AND AI-SPECIFIC ROLES

A Note on the Shifting Technology Landscape

Before getting into who builds what and who sits where, it is worth considering why these roles matter at all. The technology is moving quickly, and the firms that get value from it are the ones that have people inside the building who understand it well enough to shape how it gets used. Those people do not appear by accident. Someone has to hire them, train them, give them room to work, and decide where in the org chart they sit.

The rest of this section is about how to think through those choices. While there is a chapter in this book dedicated to tool selection (see chapter 7), it is worth briefly addressing here a question that firms are grappling with right now: namely, how much should we commit to particular AI tools and for how long? The industry has long framed this as 'build versus buy', but neither term captures what is actually happening. Building implies permanence; buying implies ownership. In a market that is moving this fast, neither is advisable for most AI tooling. The better analogy is renting (see the 'Build, Buy, or Rent' section in chapter 7).

It is important to keep your core infrastructure in excellent order, particularly your document management systems or enterprise search, because those are long-term commitments you cannot easily walk away from. They are the foundations of the building. But treat AI tools as plug-and-play. This means you should invest lightly, keep things transferable, and avoid attaching too much to the walls of any single platform; one should not renovate one's kitchen if one is on a twelve-month lease. The tools will change. The vendors will change. The capabilities will change. A workflow that feels indispensable today may be superseded by a platform update next quarter.

Firms that build deep integrations with a single AI provider, customizing extensively and embedding the tool into every part of their operation, may find that the switching costs become untenable precisely at the moment when a better option arrives. The firms that fare best will be the ones that kept their commitments light, their data portable, and their workflows reproducible across platforms. You *are* going to move. The question is when and where, not whether you will.

The pace of change is only accelerating, and the pattern so far has been one of successive expansions in capability. Modern legal AI began with point solutions such as Kira and Luminance, which targeted specific tasks such as contract review and due diligence with narrow, purpose-built models. Then came end-to-end workbench tools such as Harvey and Legora, offering more expansive platforms capable of handling a wider range of legal work within a single environment. Now, general-purpose development tools such as Anthropic's Claude and Google's Gemini put powerful capability directly in the hands of lawyers and technologists without requiring a legal AI vendor as intermediary.

Each phase has not necessarily replaced the one before it so much as expanded the range of what is possible and who can build it. What was once only accessible through a dedicated vendor may soon be buildable by a capable legal engineer or LegalQuant[1] with the right foundation model and the right data. Whether that means fewer vendors, different vendors, or a fundamentally different relationship between firms and the platforms they use is still playing out. What is clear is that assumptions firms made even twelve months ago about which tools would anchor their AI strategy may not hold. We return to this issue in detail later in the book, but the reason it matters here is that the roles a firm needs, and the skills it should be hiring for, depend entirely on where this evolution lands.

AI-Enabling Roles

Several functions within a firm play a critical enabling role, even though their primary mandate is not related to AI itself. The general counsel and risk teams assess what tools can be deployed, under what conditions, and with what safeguards. They are also asked to evaluate new features, new use cases, and client restrictions on an almost rolling basis. Data privacy professionals are increasingly in demand, not only from the firms but also from clients seeking advice on their own AI adoption. Information governance teams ensure that the data feeding AI tools is appropriately classified, secured, and compliant. IT teams deal with the architecture in which AI tools sit and how they integrate with other software. These are not AI roles in the traditional sense, but without them, responsible deployment is impossible.

These functions are also generating new business. As noted in the previous chapter, firms are increasingly being asked by clients to advise on AI governance, draft AI use policies, and consult on tool selection and data privacy risk. What begins as an internal compliance function can become a client-facing advisory service (see 'Advising Clients on AI as a Distinct Service Line' in chapter 3). This extends beyond simple tick-box responses to requests for proposals (RFPs) on how firms are using AI, generally. Some firms are offering genuine consulting engagements, helping clients strategize about AI adoption, running innovation workshops, and co-designing operational frameworks.

AI-Specific Roles

The early wave of generative AI created demand for 'prompt engineers' (individuals skilled at writing effective instructions for a language model), but that demand has largely dissipated. What has replaced it is a broader category of 'AI engineers', 'legal engineers', or, now, the emerging 'LegalQuants'. All of these terms refer to professionals who very thoroughly understand both the technology and the legal context in which it is being applied (see chapter 9). These individuals configure tools, build workflows, design prompts and personas, and sit at the intersection of legal practice and technology capability. They are a subject matter expert in both a specific legal practice area and the technology they apply to it to solve bespoke problems. These people are truly rare powerhouses and represent an elegant evolution of the T-shaped persona.[2]

Some firms have also seen the emergence of vendor-specific roles. There have been recent instances of firms hiring specialists dedicated to a single AI platform, responsible for ensuring that lawyers are getting the most out of a particular tool. Vendors themselves have introduced embedded positions such as 'innovation partners' or forward-deployed innovators, placed as the face of the product, to support a customer firm's adoption after sale. This model reflects an acknowledgment on both sides that the investment in AI tools is significant and that meaningful adoption rates without dedicated support often fall short.

There is a tension here, however. Reliance on a vendor for both the technology and the people to run it creates dependency. If the firm builds its own workflows, it retains a proprietary advantage but bears the full burden of support and might miss the benefit of market-tested best practice. If it relies entirely on the vendor, it gains support and scalability but sacrifices control and risks lock-in. And there is a further consideration: the speed with which these tools are changing makes self-built workflows difficult to maintain. Without the team and infrastructure to keep up, bespoke solutions become outdated almost as quickly as they are deployed. That said, the release of more capable models from Anthropic and OpenAI in late 2025 and the democratization of software-as-a-service development is changing the calculus on this significantly, especially when considered in tandem with the LegalQuant persona described above. This is a burgeoning area that is worth watching closely.

DATA SCIENTISTS AND ANALYSTS

One of the clearest differentiators between firms that are leading in AI and those that are following is the presence of genuine data science capability. Firms with professionals who hold advanced qualifications in machine learning, AI, and data science are able to engage with the technology at a fundamentally deeper level. They can evaluate tools more critically, understand the implications of architectural decisions before they become industry consensus, and measure the effectiveness of deployments in meaningful ways.

To realize the full value of data in law firms, organizations need fully developed teams with a range of specialties that might include any or all of the following.

- Data architects and engineers who build the infrastructure that connects systems together and moves information between platforms.
- Data scientists who analyse patterns across matters and develop predictive models.
- Data analysts who interpret operational and financial information to support decision-making.

- Knowledge management professionals who curate legal content and maintain precedent libraries.
- Legal or knowledge engineers who translate legal logic into structured formats that can be used by technology systems.

These professionals also drive strategy in a way that generalist innovation teams cannot. They can assess emerging developments, evaluate vendor claims with technical rigour, and identify opportunities that would never surface from a purely operational perspective. At one firm, data scientists built a model to detect when time was being billed to the wrong matter, which was a problem that no off-the-shelf vendor tool was designed to solve. That project took months of iteration, testing different approaches, and refining the model, and it required exactly the kind of deep technical capability that most innovation teams lack. No vendor platform would have delivered it, and without in-house data science talent, the opportunity would never have even been identified let alone pursued.

Data science capability should be closely linked with data and information architecture, which typically sits within IT, and with data and information governance, which typically sits within risk or IT. These are distinct functions, but they must work in close coordination. The data scientists understand what the technology can do. The architects ensure that the underlying systems can support whatever that is. The governance team ensures it is done responsibly. When these three functions operate in silos, as they often do, the result is either good ideas that cannot be implemented or implemented solutions that create compliance risk.

One of the most valuable things this combined capability produces is a clear view of what is actually happening with AI inside the firm. Without data scientists, architects, and governance working together, most firms have no reliable way to see who is using which tools, on what kind of work, and to what effect. And without that information, every other decision in this chapter, from where to put AI capability to which roles to hire, ends up being made on instinct.

Measuring What Matters

You cannot manage, evaluate, or control for that which you do not measure. All of which raises the obvious next question, which is how a firm actually sees any of this clearly enough to act on it. To understand who is building, what is being used, and where the gaps lie, firms must have tools and processes to monitor AI usage. This goes beyond simple login counts. It involves understanding what types of work AI is being used for, which practices are adopting it most effectively, and where investment in training or tooling will have the greatest impact. This is discussed further in the context of governance in chapter 8, but the essential point is that measurement is not just a governance function, it is a strategic one that informs every decision about where to invest in skills, tools, and people.

SKILLS AND WHERE TO SOURCE THEM

The conversation about what lawyers need to learn has evolved rapidly. As we have already mentioned, early discussions centred on prompt engineering. While this remains relevant at a basic level, the concept has broadened significantly. The better framing is 'technology competence' or, in the terminology that is increasingly adopted by platforms, 'skill building'. This means not only knowing how to prompt a tool, but also knowing how to identify correct (and incorrect) use cases and understanding how to build personas, configure functionality, design workflows, identify hallucinations, and take advantage of a platform's capabilities in a way that goes beyond simple question-and-answer use.

The distinction matters because it shifts the role of the lawyer from passive user to active participant in how the technology works. Lawyers are not being asked to become engineers, but they are increasingly expected to understand how to shape the tools to their practice instead of waiting for a technology team to do it for them. The lawyer of the near future is less a subject matter expert who happens to use technology and more a puppetmaster of agents and tools, directing capabilities rather than simply consuming them.

PROCESS MAPPING AND SERVICE DESIGN

One of the most undervalued skills in AI deployment is the ability to map existing processes and, critically, to reimagine them. Process mapping is the foundation of workflow automation and agentic AI. If you do not understand the steps, decision points, and handoffs in a current process, you cannot automate it. And if you only automate what already exists, you miss the opportunity to design something better.

Service design – understanding who the users are, what their needs are, and how to design technology-supported processes that serve those needs – is closely related. Firms that invest in these capabilities, whether within innovation teams or embedded within practice groups, tend to find more meaningful applications for AI because they are starting from the right question. That is, 'What problem are we solving?' Without that discipline, firms risk chasing the next piece of technology because everyone else is chasing it and then not knowing what to do with it once they have it. The lawyer is shown a tool, told it is transformative, and left to figure out the rest. Without time or guidance, they use it like a chatbot, because that was the first thing they were shown. And then the firm wonders why adoption metrics look superficial.

LAWYERS AS INNOVATORS

Perhaps the most important point in this chapter is that innovation does not originate from innovation teams. Innovation teams provide the conditions, the tools, the frameworks, and the guardrails, but the best innovations come from lawyers working with clients every day. They understand the pain points. They know the personas. They see the repetitive tasks that consume disproportionate time.

The role of a chief innovation officer, described candidly, is at best that of a chief marginal improvement officer. The job is not to innovate but to create the conditions in which innovation happens. That means empowering lawyers, making innovation part of their firm's strategy, providing sandboxes where lawyers can experiment safely, and ensuring there is a security framework and robust support around self-built tools and skills.

This requires a degree of trust. Innovation teams that try to hold everything centrally, insisting that all requests come through them or that all builds be done by them, quickly become bottlenecks. Lawyers, particularly partners who are owners of the business, will simply work around them. The most effective approach is to set guardrails, provide safe environments, and then step back. If a firm provides only an outdated sandbox, lawyers will go to Claude or ChatGPT on their own accounts. If the firm provides current, capable tools within a governed framework, lawyers are far more likely to innovate within the boundaries the firm has set. The choice is not between control and chaos. It is between governance that works with the grain of how lawyers actually behave and governance that pretends that lawyers will do as they are told.

TALKING TO CLIENTS

A growing part of the skills landscape involves client engagement. Responding to RFPs with a checklist of AI tools is no longer sufficient. As discussed, clients are asking deeper questions. They want to understand how firms are using AI and what governance frameworks are in place, and, increasingly, they are looking to their law firms for genuine consulting on their own AI strategies. This ranges from high-level briefings for in-house legal teams to full consulting engagements covering tool selection, policy drafting, and operational design. The conversation has various levels, but the ground-floor level is that every lawyer in the firm should be able to hold a credible conversation with a client about AI, what the firm is doing with it, how it affects work, and what it means for the client's business. This should not be a speciality within the firm but rather a baseline expectation for all.

SUPPLEMENTING, NOT SUPPLANTING (WITH A CAVEAT)

A word that comes up often in these discussions is 'supplementing'. AI supplements the lawyer's work. It does not replace the lawyer. This is true, and it is the right framing for most of what is happening today. But in the spirit of a true lawyer, this requires a caveat. Some roles, and some tasks within roles, will be supplanted. Some will be outsourced.[3] Junior review work that once required teams of trainees and associates can now be done faster and more consistently by AI, with fewer people. That does not mean associates become unnecessary, but it does mean that the mix of what they do will change, and the number of them needed to do it may change too. Firms that pretend otherwise risk being unprepared. The better approach is to acknowledge the shift, plan for it, and ensure that the people affected are equipped with the skills they need to move into the work that remains and grows as AI takes over the parts that were always more mechanical than intellectual.

The implications run deeper than headcount. The traditional leverage model, in which a broad base of junior lawyers performs high volumes of process-driven work, is being compressed from both ends. A transaction that once required eight associates and two partners may now require three associates, a legal engineer, and one partner. The team is smaller, the mix is different, and junior work shifts from producing first drafts to validating AI-generated ones, where the ability to spot what an output got wrong matters more than speed of production. Firms that keep hiring at historic volumes without rethinking what those lawyers will do and how they will be trained risk creating a generation of associates without a clear development pathway. Those that confront it early, through structured rotations, earlier client exposure, and dedicated time for working with AI under supervision, will be better positioned. That same compression also dismantles the supervision process that turned juniors into experts, which raises a harder question. How do you train a lawyer when the work that used to teach them is no longer there? We take up this discussion later, in chapter 6.

IN PRACTICE

In a Sentence

Getting the structure right for effective AI use is the difference between moving faster with confidence and producing duplication, obstructive internal politics, and opportunities for shadow AI.

What to Remember

» Where AI lives determines who selects tools, who supports them, who trains lawyers on them, and who ensures they are deployed responsibly.

» Knowledge/Innovation/AI should report under one leader. Where they do not, different leaders tend to claim the same territory, producing competing agendas rather than coordinated action.

» An AI Committee is more than a governance body. Ideally composed of both practising lawyers and business teams, it should be the one group with a real view of how AI is reshaping work, leverage, and economics across the firm.

» Innovation does not originate with the innovation team. It originates with the lawyers who understand their work well enough to see where technology would change it. The innovation function's job is to set guardrails, build safe environments, and then support the practising lawyers.

» While AI primarily supports existing work, some roles, and some tasks within roles, will be supplanted. Planning for that shift openly and preparing for the future is kinder and more effective than pretending otherwise.

What to Do with This

» Before you design the organizational chart, decide who has authority over priorities, tool selection, and deployment standards, and make sure the reporting lines match where decisions get made.

» The AI Committee should be composed of practising lawyers and business services professionals. The committee's legitimacy depends on speaking for the firm as a whole. For in-house, legal should be part of the organization's AI Committee.

» Build measurement in from the start. Without visibility into who is using which tools on what work and what the results of their use are, every subsequent decision about skills, investment, and structure becomes a guess.

Questions to Sit With

» Who directs AI priorities and moves initiatives forward in your organization? Who *should* it be?

» Are you investing in people who understand both the technology and the practice, or relying on a function that understands one and not the other?

» Which of the roles, workflows, or tasks that AI will shrink are currently the ones that teach your juniors how the work gets done? What is the plan to replace that learning?

CHAPTER 5

Data Is the Work Product

If you ask lawyers where they spend the most time, the answer would probably be Outlook and Word. It is therefore easy to think that documents are the stock in trade of the legal profession, but law firms work in matters, not documents.

That distinction sounds minor, but it has profound implications for how the profession thinks about data. For years, knowledge management in law firms has been organized around individual items: a document, a precedent, a clause, a pitch proposal. Each item is catalogued, tagged, and stored. Each lives in its own silo. The result is a profession that manages its knowledge at the item level while delivering its work at the matter level. The gap between those two levels is where value is lost.

A matter is not simply a collection of documents. A matter is the legal advice that can be evidenced by documents, process flows, time and billing narratives, email correspondence, financial data, and the accumulated intelligence generated through the handling of the work. Truly understanding a matter requires seeing all of these elements as a coherent whole. Yet most firms cannot do this. They can find a precedent or locate a template, but what they cannot do, in most cases, is see the full architecture of a completed matter and understand how every component fits together. What is more, clients often look to law firms for their horizontal view of many matters across their practice, yet most law firms do not have dashboards that can easily show 'what's market' for a specific question in a given fact-pattern. Some might not yet have fully evolved their thinking of 'knowledge' as a data type, and in those instances it shows.

Going beyond the practice of law, there is substantial data around the business and operations of law that can drive insights for legal and leadership teams. Data from financial systems, time recording software, office-access-card records, intranet usage, and staffing allocation tools are all pieces of a puzzle that can provide AI systems with the context needed to power decision-making.

This chapter argues that data, understood properly, is the work product. It is not an input to the work product, nor merely a byproduct. The structured data created through the delivery of legal services is itself a valuable asset. And in the age of generative and agentic AI, the firms that recognize this will have a decisive advantage.

ENTERING THE MATRIX

Consider the closing scene of the first *Matrix* film (arguably where the series should have ended).[1] The chosen one, Neo, has unlocked his true power and now sees the world differently. He sees the cascading green code that makes up the simulated virtual world. The falling numbers and characters that make up the code resolve into shapes, structures, and meaning. He understands what is happening because he can see the underlying architecture. Drawing this parallel is not to say that we live in a simulation, but that this exercise, in essence, is what a law firm should be able to do with its matters.

Imagine a dashboard that presents the entire composition of a matter: every document, every process step, every time entry, every billing narrative, every email thread, every piece of intelligence generated during the engagement. From that dashboard you can move between layers of detail, zooming out to see patterns across hundreds of matters or zooming in to examine the drafting of a particular clause. You can see how the matter was staffed, how it progressed, where time was spent, how the position on a topic evolved over time, and what was produced. Going further, imagine if you could interrogate all of that data in natural language.

This level of visibility is not science fiction. In other professional services industries, it is routine. Investment banks and management consultancies routinely analyse engagements in this way. Law firms, by contrast, often struggle to assemble even a partial view of what occurred and when on a completed matter.

The reason for this is historical. Most law firms built their information infrastructure gradually and independently. Document management systems manage documents. Time recording systems capture hours. Billing systems handle invoices. Email lives in Outlook (although increasingly this is brought into document management systems). Precedent banks sit in separate knowledge systems or bespoke collections. Each tool performs its function well enough, but they rarely interoperate in a way that reflects the reality of how legal work is performed. The knowledge and expertise of the law firm – the things that the client actually values – remain fragmented across systems. For in-house teams, the disparate specialist systems needed to store this knowledge might not even be available. Instead of a specialized document management system, they are relying on folder structures on local drives or using the common denominator tools of the rest of the business.

Dashboards are not enough in today's world, though. Legal teams should be seeking to go further than a single pane showing all of their data in one place (dashboards have been described as 'where data goes to die' by some commentators[2]). Simply seeing the data, even in an interactive environment, is only a first step towards the real goal of using the data a law firm possesses to drive better insights and to make changes to the way in which work is undertaken.

Imagine our fictional firm Roscoe, Jasper & Mills LLP receiving a new instruction from a client that involves the negotiation of a commercial contract. The area of law is complex and specialist. With a dashboard of accumulated data, a partner could open the dashboard, review the analytics, and dive into the data to find similar matters the firm has completed, search through the firm's lawyers to find those with the relevant experience and capacity, and drill down into pricing information. While this is useful, it is a manual lift. Even being able to ask the question and receive the answer via natural language does not necessarily enact the steps that need to happen once the information is received.

What would be more impactful is for the instruction to be received and have this trigger a series of tasks that draw upon the data. This would mean that the underlying documents could be analysed and compared with the knowledge bank of RJM to see where negotiations usually end up with such documents; an experience search could be undertaken to establish a team based on their matter histories, along with any external recognition; and an initial draft of the price that should be charged for such a matter could be calculated. This sequence could even include drafting a response email to the client outlining all of this and including a fee quote (and/or engagement letter). Data being the work product means doing something meaningful with it.

WHAT COUNTS AS DATA IN A LAW FIRM?

When lawyers hear the word 'data', many instinctively think of numbers: spreadsheets, metrics, dashboards. Perhaps they also think of lines of code (like the *Matrix*, again). In reality, though, data within a law firm is far broader than this. You will note that a key part of the data in the example above is previous agreements and clauses to drive negotiations. Almost everything produced during the delivery of legal services can be considered data, and the same is true on the business side of law, where firms generate vast amounts of operational, financial, and client-related data.

This includes documents and precedents, client pitches, awards submissions, clause libraries and standard forms, emails, time entries and narratives, process maps and decision trees, financial performance, work allocation statistics, pricing data, intranet and software usage metrics, office attendance rates, research notes, and matter metadata such as jurisdiction, industry, etc. The major data points in a law firm include

- *matter data*, such as clients, types, statuses, jurisdictions, etc.;
- *time data*, such as hours, narratives, and billing codes;
- *financial data* around billing, realization, recovery, and pricing;
- *client data* on industries, relationships, feedback, Know Your Customer (KYC) information, and engagement history;
- *knowledge data*, such as documents, playbooks, common processes and workflows, research, and training; and
- *people data* on roles, skills, workload, experience, and costs.

Each of these data points contains structured or unstructured information about how legal work is performed. Historically, much of this information was treated as incidental or irrelevant, or as being relevant only to one specialist team. The document was the lawyers' final output. Everything else existed primarily to support its creation. In an AI-driven profession, that assumption begins to change. The surrounding data becomes just as valuable as the document itself.

STRUCTURING THE DATA

To understand how data can be used effectively in the legal profession, it is helpful to look at how law firms and other professional services organizations structure their information. Most professional services organizations rely on a small number of foundational data structures that underpin their operations. These structures exist regardless of industry, although they may be labelled differently depending on context.

The most common structures include

- *client data*, which identifies the organization or individual receiving services;
- *engagement data* or *matter data*, which describes the project or issue being handled, along with any matter codes;
- *work product data*, including documents, reports, and deliverables;
- *process data*, which records how work progresses through different stages;
- *financial data*, including time entries, billing narratives, pricing structures, and profitability metrics; and
- *communication data*, covering emails, meeting notes, and client interactions.

In management consulting firms, these structures are often centred around 'engagements'. In accounting firms, they might revolve around 'assignments'. In law firms, the equivalent structure is the 'matter'. The matter becomes the container in which all other information sits. Every document, email, invoice, and research note is associated with a particular matter. When the matter concludes, the entire collection of artefacts represents the firm's accumulated knowledge about how that issue was solved or addressed.

The difficulty arises when these elements are not structured consistently. Documents might be poorly named. Time entries may contain vague billing narratives. Emails might not be linked to the correct matter. Metadata may be incomplete. The way in which the client is named or referred to might differ in each piece of software. Over time, these inconsistencies accumulate and make it difficult to analyse patterns across matters.

In a world where humans are the primary interpreters of legal information, these imperfections are tolerable. Experienced lawyers can navigate ambiguity and reconstruct the story of a matter from incomplete records. Artificial intelligence is less forgiving. AI systems function better with structured and reliable inputs. Even agents, who can increasingly comprehend and understand context in the way a human can, find their process much more streamlined if the data is in a good state. If the data feeding those systems is inconsistent or incomplete, the outputs become unreliable as well.

DATA: THE NEW OIL?

For years, commentators called data 'the new oil'. The metaphor captures the fact that data can be extracted, refined, and monetized. Organizations that possess large datasets can create powerful digital services using this data. You need only think of the largest providers of legal research to see how data can be used to drive a business. Likewise, there are risks with data as there are with oil. The biggest potential issues occur on transfer, with data privacy and the location of data both being key considerations when using technology.

But the metaphor is no longer quite right. When we talk about data today, to our minds it is much more like the new uranium. Handled carefully, it can produce extraordinary amounts of power. Handled carelessly, it can create serious harm. AI systems are built on huge amounts of data, and they are leading to multi-million dollar valuation businesses. Investment in legal technology is higher than ever.[3] But when it goes wrong, it can be catastrophic. Agents are being given access to more sources of knowledge and have more control over how that is used and where it is deployed, meaning that the potential for AI to affect sensitive data is much higher than ever before.

DATA'S HIDDEN DANGERS

The hidden dangers of data are real. Poor or incomplete data produces poor results. Biased data produces biased outcomes. What this leads to is systems that are presenting incorrect answers with alarming confidence. This presents a particular challenge for lawyers because their professional duty centres on accuracy.

Bias can creep into training data through historical precedent. Certain clauses might reflect outdated assumptions. Litigation data may encode systemic biases in enforcement patterns. Even billing narratives might contain skewed representations of how legal work is distributed across teams. AI does not inherently correct these patterns. It amplifies them. This means that the quality, structure, and governance of legal data become not merely technical issues but professional responsibilities.

That potential for harm is amplified with AI agents. AI tools are already transforming legal workflows. Lawyers use them to summarize documents, draft clauses, and conduct research. When errors occur in this environment, they are usually visible. A hallucinated case citation appears. A clause is slightly incorrect. A precedent is misapplied. A competent lawyer reviewing the output can identify and correct the problem, and the systems assist with this by showing citations and underlying documents.

Agents make this review step much more difficult for lawyers. An agent executing a multistep workflow makes decisions at each stage. If the wrong information is entered at the beginning of the process, the consequences cascade through the system. This means that if an agent retrieves the wrong precedent at the start of its flow, then it is going to perform analysis based on that precedent, draft a document incorporating that analysis, and generate an email to a client explaining the conclusions. In this simple process, a lawyer could go back and check the underlying precedent used. But if the system is drawing from hundreds of precedents to track what is a 'market' position in a negotiation, it becomes incredibly difficult to find where the agent made a misstep. Each step builds on the last. By the time a human reviews the final output, the error may be embedded across multiple layers of reasoning.

However, agents will also provide solutions. Consider the problem of context. Today, using AI tools often requires moving documents out of the systems where they live and uploading them into standalone tools, stripping away metadata and matter context in the process. Agents and Model Context Protocol (see the sections below) might allow AI to operate where the data already resides, preserving that context and improving results.

This is why data infrastructure becomes critical in an agentic world. If the agent is navigating from point A to point B to point C, the underlying data must be reliable at every stage. Documents must be properly classified. Metadata must be accurate. Process flows must reflect how work actually happens.

MODEL CONTEXT PROTOCOL (MCP)

Changing the Legal Data Landscape

One reason the legal research companies have maintained such powerful positions in the legal ecosystem is their possession of vast proprietary datasets. Case law databases, editorial annotations, citators, practical guidance materials, and regulatory updates form immense curated knowledge repositories. These companies did not simply build search engines that could find things among that data, they structured it consistently and became the single points of truth for the profession.

Because these things are powered by data, AI only increases the value of such data assets. When a model is connected to a high-quality legal dataset, it becomes dramatically more useful. The difference between a generic AI model and one connected to curated legal knowledge is immediately apparent in the reliability of its outputs and its ability to look for citations. It is something that has driven a large number of partnerships or mergers within the profession, as companies that established an early foothold in the AI market searched for data to power their systems for the future. In this sense, the traditional legal information providers have been building the fuel for legal AI for decades.

But this position may not be permanent.

The Opening of Legal Data

Emerging interoperability standards such as MCP have the potential to change the balance of power in legal information. MCP allows AI systems to connect dynamically to external tools and data sources. Instead of relying solely on the data embedded in a single platform, an AI agent can retrieve information from multiple systems in real time.

For law firms, this opens up intriguing possibilities. Instead of relying exclusively on external publishers' datasets, firms could connect AI systems directly to their own internal data and use their precedent banks, their matter histories, their negotiation strategies, and their industry knowledge to enhance their delivery of legal services. In effect, the firm's own experience becomes an AI-accessible knowledge base.

MCP connections wrap around existing connectors between technologies but are much more flexible. At present, most technologies are connected by application programming interfaces (APIs). APIs are basically a way to connect technologies. MCP on the other hand is a way of connecting *artificial intelligence* to a technology, with all the ensuing adaptability that doing that will provide. Just as law firms could look at data sources beyond the research providers, in-house teams could combine knowledge from multiple panel firms and from external knowledge providers in a much more cost-effective way. This would allow them to bring more work in house and reduce costs. The implications are significant. AI might allow law firms and in-house teams to operationalize their own knowledge in entirely new ways.

THE CLIENT DATA PROBLEM

A significant challenge for law firms seeking to use their historical data to support AI development comes from client confidentiality obligations. Law firms are required to protect client information, and, in some matters, ethical walls are established so that only authorized individuals may access certain information. A further difficulty arises where clients do not permit their data to be combined with data from other clients for the purpose of developing or training AI tools or workflows. This limits the ability of firms to use their own historical work to build effective AI systems.

There is somewhat of a contradiction here. Clients frequently instruct law firms precisely because those firms possess deep experience in a particular area. A firm may be chosen because it has acted on dozens of similar transactions or disputes. Firms are increasingly structuring themselves around the industries they work with instead of the practices to which lawyers belong. Yet those same clients impose strict limits on how the resulting work product can be used and leveraged.

As mentioned above, many clients prohibit the use of their documents as training data for AI models. Others permit internal analysis but forbid external model training. Some require explicit consent before any reuse of materials. Clients want lawyers with experience drawn from many matters, but the legal profession is ethically and contractually limited in how it can aggregate and reuse the data generated by those matters. Navigating this will be one of the defining governance challenges of legal AI.

This tension around client data is extending beyond documents and into the tools used to produce them. Some clients now regard the prompts and workflows used on their projects as their intellectual property. The logic in wanting to reuse prompts from a firm's perspective is that if it takes the trouble to develop a tailored series of prompts to handle a client's regulatory filings or transaction structure, those prompts were shaped by the client's data, refined through the client's feedback, and built around the client's specific needs. For the firm, those prompts may feel like reusable institutional knowledge. For the client, they are inseparable from the engagement itself. As prompts become more sophisticated and more central to how legal work is delivered, this question will only sharpen.

Some solutions will involve anonymization and aggregation, stripping data of identifying details so that it can be used in the aggregate without exposing any individual client's information. Others may involve synthetic datasets, meaning artificially generated data that mirrors the structure and patterns of real legal work without containing any actual client information, or secure retrieval architectures that allow a model to access relevant documents at the point of use without permanently ingesting them into its training data. The approaches will vary, but the principle will remain that legal data carries obligations as well as opportunities.

BUILDING DATA TEAMS IN LAW

Though there is a thorough discussion of this topic in chapter 4, some points are worth mentioning here. Data teams need both people and a platform. As when they select any enterprise software, organizations must decide how best to procure their data platform (see the section 'Build, Buy, or Rent' in chapter 7). This is a particular challenge within the legal profession, where the importance of data has historically been underestimated, resulting in disconnected platforms and systems that were built without an overarching data strategy. As a result, many firms are now developing or refining enterprise data strategies and increasing investment in data as a core asset. Establishing a single source (or at least several clearly defined sources) of truth makes it significantly easier to apply AI to that data.

Many law firms have begun to develop dedicated data capabilities. These teams typically sit at the intersection of several functions: technology, knowledge management, innovation, and legal operations. Depending on their size, in-house teams might fold these roles into a dedicated legal operations function or might have an individual who is solely responsible for data. Their role is to transform accumulated information into usable intelligence.

This is consistent with a broader shift within the legal profession to recognize 'data' as a core technology competency for modern legal teams. Data literacy is no longer solely the domain of IT professionals; instead it is becoming a foundational capability within multidisciplinary legal teams. Lawyers, legal engineers, data analysts, and technologists increasingly collaborate to structure, interpret, and operationalize the information generated during legal work.

AI accelerates this trend. Lawyers alone cannot design or maintain the data architecture required for advanced AI systems. They might be able to vibe code alone (see chapter 9), but they require support and assistance for the rollout, architecture, and data connections. The profession, therefore, finds itself moving towards a model in which legal expertise is integrated with data science, engineering, and technology design.

DATA AS THE DIFFERENTIATOR

For much of the modern era, law firms differentiated themselves primarily through expertise and relationships. And those things still definitely matter. But AI introduces a new dimension of competition. The firms that thrive in the next decade will not simply be those that have the most sophisticated AI tools. Those tools are rapidly commoditizing across not just law firms but every department of every business across the world.

The true differentiator will be the quality and accessibility of the data that those tools can access. Every tool discussed in this book, every workflow, every agent, and every platform depends on the quality and structure of the data it works with. Those who invest in data strategy now will be positioned to take advantage of every future development. A legal team with clean, structured, matter-level data can build AI systems that understand how the firm's lawyers actually practise. It can analyse patterns across deals, disputes, and negotiations. It can surface insights that were previously buried inside millions of documents. A team with fragmented, poorly structured data will struggle to achieve the same results. Firms that do not invest in data will find themselves perpetually limited, owning powerful tools that underperform because the data feeding them is inadequate.

IN PRACTICE

In a Sentence

The competitive advantage in an AI-enabled practice belongs to organizations that treat the matter, not the document, as the unit of knowledge and understand how to operationalize it.

What to Remember

» A matter is not a stack of documents. It is the totality of legal advice evidenced by documents, process flows, time and billing narratives, emails, financial data, and the accumulated intelligence produced along the way. Most teams cannot currently see any given matter as a whole.

» Ensure your systems (document management, time recording, matter management) talk to each other.

» Agents raise the stakes of poor data quality. One wrong precedent retrieved at the start of a multistep workflow cascades errors into analysis, drafting, and client communication before a human sees it.

» Model Context Protocol (MCP) lets firms more intelligently connect AI systems directly to their own precedent banks, matter histories, negotiation records, and industry knowledge.

» Client confidentiality and data-reuse restrictions create a real tension. Working out what you can anonymize, aggregate, or retain for internal improvement is one of the defining governance questions of the next few years.

What to Do with This

» Map where your data lives and whether the different repositories are reconcilable. Document management, time entries, billing narratives, emails, and matter metadata systems must all speak to each other for an agent to navigate them reliably.

- Before deploying agents, invest in data governance. That means accurate document classification, metadata you can trust, matter records that link to each other, and process documentation that reflects how work happens.
- Negotiate explicit data policies with your clients. Say what you can and cannot reuse, anonymize, aggregate, or retain for internal AI improvement.
- Build a data team with real breadth: architects to connect systems, scientists to find patterns, analysts to interpret operational information, knowledge professionals to curate content, and legal engineers to translate legal logic into structured form.

Questions to Sit With

- If you deployed an agent tomorrow with access to every matter file you have ever opened, would that data be clean enough and structured enough for the agent to retrieve the right precedent reliably?
- What do your current client engagement letters say about reusing experience gained from a matter, and what do they need to say?
- Who in your organization currently owns data strategy from end to end, and does that person have the authority to make decisions that cross IT, knowledge, and practices?

CHAPTER 6

Adoption, Engagement, and Training

Without meaningful adoption, innovation is a meaningless pursuit, and driving such adoption takes a village.

Selecting tools, developing strategy, and building technical infrastructure are only the opening gambits in the transformation of legal work. The real challenge begins afterwards. It begins when lawyers must truly change how they work, how they learn, and how they develop judgement in a profession that has historically been shaped by apprenticeship and repetition.

This chapter addresses two related questions.

- How do law firms and legal teams train lawyers to use AI and other emerging technologies effectively?
- How do we train the next generation of lawyers when the traditional training model is being reshaped by automation?

These questions are not theoretical. Innovation teams in law firms encounter them every day. The legal sector has spent decades introducing new tools with the promise of disruption only to discover that adoption is not as widespread as expected. A tool can be powerful, the strategy supporting it can be thoughtful, and the business cases for its use can be compelling, but none of these things matter if lawyers do not use the tool in their day-to-day work and, perhaps more importantly, if they do not understand when and how it should be used.

Lawyers are not natural early adopters. Their professional training emphasizes risk identification, reliance on precedent, and caution. They are also extraordinarily busy. Add to this the fact that many lawyers have previously experienced 'transformational' technologies that failed to deliver, and it becomes easier to understand why adoption is often slow. When technology is introduced into that environment, it competes not only with scepticism but also with the simple pressure of time.

Training and engagement therefore become central components of innovation, not peripheral activities or optional support functions. They are the mechanism through which change actually happens.

AI AS BOTH PROBLEM AND SOLUTION

Chapter 4 ended with discussion of the leverage model and the shrinking base of junior work. This chapter takes up the question that follows from those issues: how do you train a lawyer when the work that used to teach them is no longer there? AI presents the profession with an unusual situation: it gives rise to real issues in training future legal professionals while also being the tool that could ultimately solve those issues.

AI as Problem

So what is the problem with AI when it comes to training lawyers? In short, the tasks AI is best at are the ones junior lawyers used to cut their teeth on: reviewing documents in data rooms, working through due diligence, running research, pulling document sets together, proofreading long stacks of documents to catch inconsistencies or risk allocation problems. None of this is glamorous, and a lot of it is closer to administrative work than to anything junior lawyers learned in law school. But doing all of it, over and over, is how juniors learn to become 'real' lawyers. By the time a junior is advising clients, they have seen enough matters and enough documents to understand how the pieces fit together.

A junior associate who spends weeks reviewing transaction documents begins to recognize patterns. They learn how contracts fit together. They develop attention to detail and professional discipline. Most importantly, they gain context. By the time they are asked to advise a client directly, they have already encountered dozens of similar issues.

AI increasingly performs these tasks in minutes, or even seconds. From a productivity perspective, this development is extraordinary. Lawyers can take on much more work and complete simple tasks quickly at any level of seniority. From a training perspective, though, it raises difficult questions. If the machine conducts the due diligence, where does the junior lawyer learn how due diligence works? If AI produces the first draft of a tricky clause, how does the lawyer learn nuance? This is a genuine problem, and it is not solved by simply handing the associate an AI tool and telling them to supervise it.

The question we are asking now is how new lawyers will navigate the complexities of legal practice without these formative experiences. The concern that many within the profession are voicing is if AI removes the repetition, does it also remove the learning? If AI accelerates the work but bypasses the human practice, how will the juniors of today become the experts of tomorrow?

These questions extend beyond drafting. If AI summarizes research, will lawyers learn to read cases critically? If AI suggests contractual amendments, will lawyers develop the judgement required to assess whether those amendments are appropriate? And perhaps most importantly, what if the technology fails or produces misleading output? Will the lawyers be able to catch the inevitable machine errors?

These are not uniquely legal concerns. Medicine, accounting, engineering, and journalism are grappling with similar issues. Across professions, AI is most useful when used by experienced practitioners who can evaluate its output quickly. Yet those practitioners were once juniors themselves. They became experts through years of practice.

One answer is that this is simply how work evolves, and the profession needs to move with the times. Plenty of skills that used to be foundational are now obsolete, and no one mourns them. And that might turn out to be true here too. But the tasks AI is taking over are not narrow technical skills, they are the everyday repetitions that taught a generation of lawyers how the work actually fits together. Until the profession finds another way to build that foundation, the gap is real; pretending otherwise will not close it.

AI as Solution

AI is the impetus for revamping the training model, but it might also be the solution to the problem it creates. Firms can use AI to create simulation environments that replace learning-by-doing with learning-by-simulating. Just as pilots must have a certain amount of simulator hours to fly a plane, a junior lawyer can run simulated M&A negotiations against an AI opponent, learning deal strategy, negotiation tactics, and the rhythm of a transaction in compressed time. They can use AI to practise drafting, receiving immediate feedback on their work without waiting for a partner's redline. They can use AI as a mentor, asking the questions they are afraid to ask a real partner, building understanding through iteration.

In educational settings, this approach is already emerging. Several universities have begun experimenting with AI-based teaching avatars. At Georgia Tech, for example, Professor David Joyner has created an AI system trained on his lecture notes, published articles, and teaching materials.[1] Students can interact with these digital assistants outside classroom hours, asking questions about their course or about hypothetical scenarios. The system responds in a manner consistent with the professor's approach to teaching. The idea is not to replace the professor but to extend the learning environment beyond the classroom.

A similar model could emerge in law firms. Imagine a junior associate interacting with a 'digital twin', or 'avatar', trained on a partner's historical drafting style and deal preferences. The associate could ask questions about the matter or about their practice area and receive answers that might replicate informal mentorship conversations.

This is helpful because one of the most common themes raised by junior lawyers is anxiety about asking questions. Law is a profession where competence is often associated with confidence. Admitting uncertainty can feel risky. AI removes that social barrier. A junior lawyer can ask basic questions without fear of appearing uninformed. They can build foundational understanding before approaching their supervising partner with more targeted queries. Rather than replacing the human mentor, the AI makes the human mentoring relationship more productive by ensuring the junior arrives at the conversation with enough context to benefit from it.

Educational theory reinforces this theory of effectiveness. Back in 1984 Benjamin Bloom compared classroom teaching and mastery learning (where the student reaches mastery in one topic before moving onto the next) to one-to-one mentoring.[2] What he discovered was that the average tutored student performed better than about 98% of classroom-taught students. Bloom argued that individual tutoring is the most effective form of teaching because it allows

- immediate feedback,
- adaptive pacing,
- personalized explanations, and
- continuous diagnosis of misunderstandings.

With AI mentoring there is an opportunity for training to be closer to the mentoring model, and therefore to be more effective than existing training methods.

LAW SCHOOLS AND THE CHANGING TRAINING MODEL

Understanding Law Schools

The training burden does not fall solely on law firms. Law schools face a fork in the road. They cannot remain purely academic institutions divorced from the realities of practice. The profession must build a bridge between academic education and the practical demands of the work.

'Law school' is a broad term and it is worth defining what is meant, particularly because the concept differs between jurisdictions. In the United States, law is a postgraduate educational choice. Students therefore attend law school with the clear intention of entering the legal profession, and close links to the profession are both expected and necessary. In England and Wales, however, law can be studied at both undergraduate and postgraduate level. Postgraduate law schools are closer in nature to the US model as those attending are generally headed towards the profession, whether as solicitors or barristers. Universities delivering undergraduate law degrees find themselves in a more complicated position as students may want to qualify as solicitors within law firms, become court-facing barristers in chambers, pursue other careers, or simply study law as an academic subject. Close links with the profession can therefore risk alienating part of the student body.

For clarity, when we talk about law schools in this book we are referring to postgraduate law schools, where those entering are most likely to be headed towards becoming employed as a lawyer.

A Transatlantic Perspective: UK and US Legal Education

The difference between the UK and US legal education systems highlights the complexity of the debate surrounding modernization of legal education. In the United States, the Juris Doctor (JD) is primarily an academic qualification. Students study doctrinal subjects, participate in moot courts, and sometimes engage in clinical programmes that simulate practice. However, newly qualified lawyers typically enter practice immediately after graduation and passing the bar exam.

The United Kingdom has historically adopted a more explicitly staged approach. Students complete an academic law degree (or law conversion course following the completion of another subject at undergraduate level), followed by professional training and then a two-year training contract, during which they generally rotate through practice areas under supervision.

The introduction of the Solicitors Qualifying Examination (SQE) in England and Wales in 2021 changed this landscape. The SQE replaced the previous Legal Practice Course (LPC) with a centralized assessment system and introduced the concept of Qualifying Work Experience (QWE). Instead of a rigid training contract structure, aspiring solicitors can now gain qualifying experience across multiple organizations, including law firms, in-house teams, legal clinics, and alternative legal service providers. The LPC, however, remains relevant because it is the form of education that the most senior lawyers within an organization remember and it colours how they think of education.

The SQE provides law schools with significantly greater flexibility than they had under the old system when it comes to designing their programmes. Law schools can now integrate practical training, technological literacy, and interdisciplinary skills in ways that were previously constrained by regulatory requirements. For example, some institutions are now experimenting with technology-enhanced legal clinics, where students use AI-assisted research tools to support real clients under supervision. Others incorporate courses on legal data analytics, legal design, or automation.[3]

The SQE therefore opens a window for innovation in legal education. Law schools can experiment with new training models while still ensuring that graduates meet a consistent professional standard through the centralized exam.

In the United States, similar experimentation is emerging through interdisciplinary programmes that combine law with computer science, data science, or business analytics. Northwestern Pritzker School of Law, for example, has collaborated with engineering and computer science faculties to expose law students to emerging legal technologies.

How Law Schools Evolve

One model suggests that law schools should integrate hands-on technical training alongside traditional legal education. Students should graduate not only understanding the law but also understanding how to use the tools that will define their practice. This model has the advantage of immediacy as graduates arrive at firms ready to work with AI tools from day one.

An alternative model, more closely aligned with investment banking, suggests that law schools remain as they are: that is, academic institutions focused on legal reasoning, statutory interpretation, and the foundations of the profession. The practical training then happens at the firm in the form of a structured supervisory training scheme that precedes independent practice. In England and Wales this model already exists in the form of a mandatory training period before qualification, although, as discussed, since the SQE was introduced this can be completed across multiple employers. In the United States the transition would be more dramatic, but the principle that we should separate the academic from the practical and structure each deliberately is the same. Another alternative is to make use of formalized apprenticeship structures. In England and Wales the solicitor apprenticeship pathway is an approved method of qualification and it provides flexibility for on-the-job learning that could start directly from secondary school/high school or after an undergraduate degree.

Embedding AI into learning means using some form of technology. Although law schools will attempt to be tool agnostic, the competition for influence over the next generation of lawyers is already underway. Tools such as Harvey and Legora are taking their rivalry into law schools, offering tool-specific training and building relationships with students before they enter the profession. Under this model, students will graduate not only with substantive legal knowledge but also with practical familiarity with legal technologies, data analysis tools, and AI-assisted research platforms.

The vendors understand that the tools students use at law school will shape the tools they advocate for as associates. This turf battle will influence which platforms dominate in firms over the next decade, and it means that law school training is no longer a purely academic question, it is also a commercial one.

NEW SKILLS

This is not just about using technology, though. The introduction of AI requires practitioners to learn new skills or evolve existing skills. While law schools are used to teaching resilience, it is just as important that lawyers become comfortable with ongoing change. AI tools are moving rapidly. Features are being introduced every week, user interfaces are changing, and the back-end models that power the tools are being updated constantly. This is not a pace of change that lawyers are used to.

Another skill that has to evolve is the art of verification. Law schools already know how to teach this in a research context, where the rule is to rely on primary sources, but AI tool outputs make that harder. They sound right, and they produce work that is convincing enough that there have already been instances of lawyers filing briefs that cite cases that do not exist. For law schools trying to figure out how to teach students to use these tools, the challenge involves rebuilding the habits of verification for a world where the thing you are checking was written by something that does not know whether it is telling the truth.

These developments suggest that the boundary between legal education and professional training may become increasingly porous. Whether or not law schools evolve, firms will need to invest in structured early-career development. If newly minted lawyers are learning practical skills at the firm instead of at school, difficult questions follow. Are their salaries the same as current first-year associates? Are clients paying for their time? For how long? These are not rhetorical questions. They have direct implications for firm economics and for how the early years of legal practice are structured.

FROM YEARS TO LEVELS: ACCELERATED PROGRESSION

The traditional associate model involves progression in a 'lock-step' fashion. Associates progress through years of post-qualification experience, and their seniority is tied to time served. Eventually, they may be selected for the 'partnership track', where they are groomed for entering the partnership. In an age of AI, this model is overdue for reconsideration. AI does not merely change what associates do, it changes how quickly they can develop.

The emerging model is competency-based rather than time-based. Instead of first year, second year, third year, firms might increasingly adopt level 1, level 2, level 3 designations tied to demonstrated capability instead of calendar time. Associates accelerated by AI simulation training can reach substantive competency in months rather than years. They will not spend three years doing due diligence and eDiscovery. They will work through foundational tasks quickly, demonstrate their capability, and begin doing real substantive work far sooner.

This acceleration cuts both ways. For associates who thrive, the path to meaningful work becomes dramatically shorter. For those who lack the judgement, analytical capacity, or work ethic that the profession demands, the assessment happens much faster. Where traditional progression allowed weaknesses to be masked by the sheer volume of routine work, the accelerated model surfaces capability gaps quickly. Firms will be able to determine within months whether an associate has the qualities needed to progress instead of that process taking years.

Associates themselves will also self-select more quickly. A junior lawyer who realizes within six months that the work is not what they want to do for a living has a different career calculus than one who makes the same realization after three years. The accelerated model is more honest, if also more intense.

The implications for firm economics are significant. If associates reach partnership-track capability faster, the traditional leverage model changes. Fewer junior associates doing more substantive work but at higher rates replaces large teams of juniors doing routine work at lower rates. This connects us directly back to the business model questions discussed in chapter 3.

ALTERNATIVE PATHS

The partnership track is no longer the only path available. Technology providers are recruiting directly from law firms[4] and law firms are opening up multidisciplinary routes for 'AI lawyers' and 'innovation lawyers'. Evidence of this change can be seen in the sheer number of jobs available when searching for such terms on job sites.[5] Many have built out innovation or AI functions that might operate either as traditional business services teams or as practice areas in and of themselves. There is no longer only one path to advancement.

While everyone in the firm must have a working knowledge of AI and a baseline level of AI literacy, those who choose to specialize in this area will be as important as those who choose to specialize in a particular legal practice. Some law firms are already rewarding people in this way, and there are numerous partners within firms who are leading innovation teams. There will only be more diversification of legal teams in the future as those with technology skills are paired with pure legal practitioners in order to deliver legal advice.

LEADERSHIP TRAINING: THE KNOWLEDGE GAP AT THE TOP

AI has very quickly arrived everywhere all at once, and this is exposing a lack of knowledge within firms' leadership teams. The following example, which has been shared with the authors, showcases why this is a problem. A first-year associate at a large firm wanted to use AI to clean up a witness transcript (for grammar issues, punctuation, and so on). The associate had typed it nearly verbatim from a recorded interview and wanted to use AI to finalize it before sending it to the witness for review. They told their supervising senior attorney what they intended to do and the senior attorney did not see a problem.

But in a litigation context, using AI to revise a witness transcript from what was actually said to a cleaned-up version raises serious concerns. The substance of what the witness said matters.[6] Changing it, even to improve readability, risks altering meaning in ways that could affect the case. The problem was not the junior lawyer's initiative, it was that the senior lawyer did not know enough about the tool, or about the implications of its use in that context, to identify the risk and say no.

Partners and supervising attorneys must understand proper and improper use cases for AI tools even if they do not use those tools themselves every day. They do not need to be power users. They need to know what the tools do, where they excel, and where their use is inappropriate or dangerous. This is a change management project for how the firm operates.

Indeed, leaders need to be trained not only on tools but on change management itself. Lawyers are not, as a group, natural change agents. They are trained in precedent, in stability, in the careful management of risk. Asking them to champion new ways of working requires more than a demonstration. It requires equipping them with the skills and confidence to drive behavioural change across their teams. If the partners and supervising attorneys are not championing these new ways of working, nothing will stick.

TEACHING JUDGEMENT, NOT JUST TECHNOLOGY

The core challenge in AI training is not teaching people how to use a tool, it is teaching judgement about when to use which tool, when to use tools in tandem, when a task still needs manual intervention despite being automatable, and when a tool's output needs to be overridden rather than accepted. This is not just a law school problem of teaching new skills, as discussed above, it is relevant for the whole profession.

This challenge is compounded by a dynamic that both vendors and firm leadership have created. Legal AI providers aspire to become the operating system of the law firm: a single environment through which all legal work flows. This aspiration is understandable from a commercial perspective, and it is also appealing to firm leadership, which is attracted to the simplicity of one system that handles everything. As one observer noted, the appeal is the same as it would be for a piece of enterprise resource planning software that integrated all core business processes (finance, HR, marketing, etc.) into one system that is able to solve any problem.

A series of mergers and acquisitions in the legal technology space serve to showcase this intent. In the early days of legal AI, Clio, a 'legal operating system' software company, acquired vLex, which had most recently launched a legal AI tool called Vincent. This was a $1 billion acquisition and, in conjunction with a $500 million fundraising drive, it led to Clio being valued at $5 billion.[7] Becoming a single platform for legal teams is big business.

But the aspiration also has downsides. These platforms have limits. They excel at certain types of work and are inappropriate for others. A disputes team would not route all of its eDiscovery work through a legal AI tool such as Harvey or Legora if the firm also uses a specific eDiscovery platform that is specifically designed for that area of law. Contractual work that requires deep, jurisdiction-specific analysis may need tools that the general platform does not offer. The point solution is not dead. It remains essential for work that requires specialized capability.

Training must therefore address not only how to use a given tool but also when the value of that tool ends and when it becomes necessary to look for or use alternative tools, including point solutions, manual processes, or simply human action and judgement. This requires a level of sophistication in training that goes well beyond the typical product demonstration. It requires ongoing education about the evolving capabilities of each tool, the relationships between tools, and the judgement to know which tool fits which situation.

ENGAGEMENT AND ADOPTION: THE INCENTIVE PROBLEM

Although substantive training is part of it, meaningful adoption also requires addressing the incentive structures that drive lawyer behaviour, and those structures are, in many cases, actively hostile to adoption.

One firm reported that following the thorough rollout of a sophisticated AI tool, their associates refused to use it until they had hit their billable hour targets for the month. Only after they had met their personal billing requirements did they have time to explore new ways of working. This is the perverse incentive problem in its purest form: the billable hour rewards time spent, not efficiency achieved. An associate who uses AI to complete a task in two hours instead of ten has produced the same work product but billed eight fewer hours. Under traditional compensation models, that associate has performed worse, not better.

This problem is well understood, and yet it persists. And it does so because the billable hour, despite all its flaws, remains the dominant metric for evaluating associate contribution. Firms have begun experimenting with alternatives. Some grant associates credit for time spent using or developing AI tools, counting it as billable contribution. Ropes & Gray, for instance, now credits first- and second-year associates with up to 400 hours of AI-related work that counts toward their billable targets, sending a clear signal that using AI is not a distraction from fee earning but a core part of professional development.[8] Other firms offer monetary incentives tied to adoption milestones.

But the problem extends beyond associates. Partners face their own version of the incentive misalignment. If a partner's practice generates significant revenue from work that AI can now perform faster or eliminate entirely, that partner has a financial disincentive to adopt. The same logic that prevents associates from using AI until they have hit their hours prevents partners from championing tools that might reduce their practice's billings.

MEASURING RETURN ON INVESTMENT: SHORT, MEDIUM, AND LONG TERM

The question of how much ROI is derived from AI tools gets asked constantly but answered badly. With most technology, working out ROI is straightforward enough. You look at what the tool costs, you look at what it saves or earns, and you see whether the second number is bigger than the first. The conversation about AI has moved quickly from 'Are you using it?' to 'What is it actually returning?', and firms are reaching for that same playbook. The problem is that the playbook assumes a tool whose costs and benefits show up in the same year, on the same matter, in the same line of the profit and loss account. AI does not behave that way, which is why the honest answer to the ROI question usually depends on how far out you are willing to look.

In the long term, the biggest return on investment is that the firm stays in business. This is not hyperbole. The pace of change in the legal market is such that firms that do not invest in AI capability today risk being uncompetitive within three to five years. Their clients will begin to question why they are paying for manual processes that competitors have automated. Their best associates will leave for firms that offer modern tools and modern ways of working. Their market position will erode – not dramatically, but steadily – in ways that become progressively harder to reverse. At this moment in time, investing in legal AI tools is overhead. It is the price of doing business. It is not going to earn the firm money in the short term and it should be treated as research and development.

The issue is that firms are not set up for this sort of long-term investment pay-off. Law firms traditionally work on a year-by-year basis, with partners receiving their equity payments at the end of the financial year. All the metrics used by the market to compare law firms against each other are also assessed on a yearly basis. The ROI discussion around AI may therefore be fundamentally miscalculated, because it measures the wrong thing. These are not revenue-generating investments that can be weighed up on a yearly basis and compared against a specific figure. They are survival investments.

In the medium term, however, returns come from two sources. First, the firm wins more work because it operates more efficiently. Clients choose firms that can deliver faster, more thoroughly, and at competitive prices. Rather than being simply a cost-saving exercise, efficiency is a competitive advantage in winning mandates. Second, the firm can command higher rates for the work that remains. When AI handles the routine, the work that still requires human expertise is, by definition, the most valuable work. It is the work that clients cannot do themselves, even with their own AI tools. It is forward-looking analysis, strategic judgement, complex negotiation, and the insurance of professional accountability. Even for the work that remains supported by AI, a premium will be placed on pointing those tools at proprietary data and knowledge that is only available to that firm.

One in-house lawyer, in a confidential conversation with the authors, put it this way. She expects that in the future she will be able to bring her law firm a full AI-generated draft and ask only for verification and insurance. She is happy to pay a premium hourly rate for that service because the total cost is a fraction of what the full process previously required. If the rate is $10,000 an hour but the engagement takes one hour instead of fifty, the client is paying dramatically less while the firm's effective hourly rate has increased dramatically. The highest reported hourly rate in the market at the time of writing is approximately $4,000. In a few years the logic of expertise-and-insurance billing suggests that rates will go considerably higher, at least as measured per hour, even if total engagement costs decline.

The framing that emerges is that firms are no longer simply providing processes, they are providing a productized combination of technology, expertise, and the institutional infrastructure to stand behind the answer. Going back to our example in chapter 1, think of this like the mechanic who fixes a car. The fix might only take five minutes, but you are paying for the sum total of that mechanic's experience and training. You are paying not for time but for proven results. And to some extent it is the same for law firms: it is the infrastructure, the firm's data, its people, its reputation, and its insurance that make the service valuable. It is not the AI tool itself but what the firm builds around it.

THE HOW: CULTURE, CHANGE MANAGEMENT, AND LOCAL ADAPTATION

For large firms, each office and each practice group is, functionally, its own little business. They each have their own culture, their own leadership, their own client relationships, and their own way of doing things. What works in one office does not necessarily work in another. What engages one practice group might leave another cold.

This means that generalized adoption programmes, e.g. a single training deck rolled out firm-wide, often fail. Successful adoption requires local champions and/or contextualized training that understands the culture of the practice group and can adapt messaging and use cases accordingly. It requires experimentation with different approaches: gamification for some groups, competition for others, and fear of being left behind for others still. The change management principles are well established but their application must be tailored to the specific culture of each team.

For in-house teams, change management is different but not necessarily simpler. On one hand, the case for adoption is easier to make, since in-house lawyers answer to a business that already wants to move faster, they are not beholden to the billable hour, and they often do similar types of work repeatedly for the same company, which makes identifying use cases more straightforward. Rolling out a single process is also easier when the team reports through a corporate hierarchy rather than a partnership, where every owner may want to do things differently. On the other hand, in-house teams are generally smaller, they are already stretched across multiple practice areas, and they are usually working with tighter budgets. Where a law firm might buy a purpose-built legal AI tool and wrap a support team around it, an in-house team is more likely to be handed whatever the business has already licensed and told to make it work.

INCENTIVES AND ENGAGEMENT

All of this comes down to a deeper question about whether change is best driven by shaking the foundations of legal practice and changing the incentive structure for adopting new technology, or by changing the approach to engagement. If the billable hour model actively discourages adoption, does it need to change before engagement programmes can succeed? Or can engagement drive enough momentum to force the incentive structure to evolve?

The honest answer is that it is unclear, and there is no silver bullet. Different organizations will reach their tipping point from different directions. Some will change incentives first and watch adoption follow. Others will build adoption momentum despite the incentives and use the resulting data to justify incentive reform. The two shifts may converge gradually, and then all at once. What is clear is that both must eventually align. A firm cannot sustain AI adoption indefinitely within an incentive structure that punishes the behaviour it is trying to encourage.

Firms must explicitly reward two things. First, mindset change and experimentation. Some firms are now giving associates credit for time spent exploring AI tools, but the same must happen for partners. If experimentation is valued, it must be valued at every level. And for partners it is more complex than giving hours credit. Partners are judged by different measures, and there needs to be a way of recognizing their contribution even if it takes away from time spent bringing in business in the short term.

Second, firms must begin measuring contributions in terms other than hours. Output quality, matter outcomes, client satisfaction, innovation contributions – these are all measurable. As more conversations open up about value-based pricing, firms must also look at value-based incentives. While they are harder to measure than hours, the profession will not make the transition by measuring only what is easy.

LOOKING AHEAD

Rather than being one-time exercises, training, engagement, and adoption are ongoing processes that evolve as the tools evolve, as the profession evolves, and as client expectations shift. The firms that treat adoption as a project with a start and end date will find themselves perpetually restarting. The firms that treat it as a continuous discipline, embedded in how the firm operates rather than layered on top, will build durable capability. A recurring theme throughout this chapter is that artificial intelligence cannot be treated as an add-on to existing systems: it must be folded into a new way of working. Lifelong learning is essential.

If AI were introduced as an optional tool used occasionally by a few enthusiasts, it would remain peripheral to the profession. Training programmes, law school curricula, and firm development structures must and will instead integrate AI into the ordinary course of legal work. The most successful organizations will not necessarily be those with the most advanced tools. They will be those that embed those tools into their culture, their workflows, and their approach to learning.

IN PRACTICE

In a Sentence

There is no innovation without adoption. Training and engagement must change how lawyers work, think, and exercise judgement. Organizations need to work on incentives, leadership capability, and culture to drive sustained adoption.

What to Remember

» AI is removing the repetitive work that used to train juniors into competent lawyers.

» AI is also the most promising tool for replacing that training. Simulation, drafting practice with feedback, and one-to-one tutoring from an AI trained on the firm's own judgement give juniors a way to learn faster and without the social cost of asking the same question multiple times.

» Better incentives are needed to reward those who can produce the same (or better) work faster.

» Training has to teach judgement, not just tool use. Knowing when to use a tool, when to override it, and when to pick up the phone is harder to teach than which buttons to press, and those things matter more too.

» Partners and general counsels need their own training. While they do not need to be power users, they do need to know where AI use is and is not appropriate or they will struggle to supervise the juniors they are responsible for and to be strategic about the use of AI.

What to Do with This

» Audit your existing training programme. If it is a one-off rollout rather than a continuous practice embedded in how the firm runs, redesign it. The tools and the work change faster than annual cycles.
» As discussed in chapter 3, align incentives with the adoption you want. Credit AI-related work towards billable targets. Treat experimentation as legitimate time not stolen time.
» Introduce simulation and feedback into junior training. Supervising AI will not teach them the same lessons as traditional training. The formative experiences have to come from somewhere.
» Run a separate training track for your senior lawyers focused on the appropriate and inappropriate uses of AI, and how to manage those using it. This must be distinct from the track for those who use the tools daily.

Questions to Sit With

» Do your compensation and promotion criteria reward the behaviour you say you want?
» If the repetitive work that used to teach your juniors has been automated, where will they learn the judgement they will eventually be paid for?
» If a senior partner told you tomorrow that they did not intend to learn anything about AI because they plan to retire in five years, what would you say back?

CHAPTER 7

Picking the Tools

TOOL SELECTION AND TECH OVERLOAD

If the previous chapters have established why AI matters to the legal profession, how it reshapes strategy, what teams and skills are needed, and why data and training are foundational, this chapter addresses a question that every firm and legal department will eventually face in practice. How do you choose the right tools?

The legal technology market is moving at a pace that has no precedent in the profession. New products launch weekly, while existing products change monthly with upgrades, new features, and major enhancements. Vendors announce partnerships, integrations, and capabilities faster than innovation teams can evaluate them. Partners forward emails from clients who have heard about a tool that will apparently make work faster and better and ask, 'Can we try it?' Sometimes, they are already piloting it with a single-seat licence provided to them by a generous and eager vendor. Associates learn about new features on LinkedIn before the firm's own innovation teams or, in some cases, the customer success leads at the software company know they exist. Meanwhile, the underlying AI models themselves are evolving, with multimodel architectures becoming the standard, and agentic capabilities arriving before most firms have finished evaluating the last generation of products.

The result is a particular kind of overload that is distinct from what law firms have experienced before. Previous generations of legal technology were largely stable. A document management system might receive one significant update per year. An eDiscovery platform would follow a predictable release cycle. Lawyers could learn how to use a tool and trust that it would work the same way next month. But that stability is gone. The tools that firms are adopting today will not be the same in six months' time, and some of the tools that firms are evaluating today will not even exist in a year.

This chapter is about navigating that reality. It is not a buyer's guide to specific products, because any such guide would be obsolete by the time you are reading this book. Instead, it sets out the processes, frameworks, and disciplines that enable firms and legal teams to make defensible decisions about technology, even in an environment that refuses to sit still.

THE STATE OF THE MARKET

Any honest assessment of the legal AI market has to begin with an admission, which is that nobody has a complete picture. The market is too large and too fragmented, and it is changing too quickly for any single person, team, or consultancy to track comprehensively. Firms that try to boil the ocean, spending significant time each day attempting to catalogue every new development, every new product, and every new partnership, are wasting resources they do not have.

That is not a counsel of ignorance but rather a counsel of efficiency. Firms should maintain a general awareness of where the market is heading and what the major categories of tools look like. They should know the difference between a platform play and a point solution; between a wrapper around a frontier model and the expanding productization coming from the frontier labs themselves; between a tool that embeds into existing workflows and one that requires lawyers to adopt an entirely new interface.

But the goal is not omniscience. The goal is to know enough to ask the right questions when a specific need arises.

There are resources that help. Legaltech Hub and similar directories catalogue and review products across the market.[1] The SKILLS community publishes data on what products are most often leveraged for different use cases, and provides information about which are the most recommended vendors.[2] Consultancies with a broad view of the market can help firms shortlist options for specific use cases without requiring every firm to conduct its own exhaustive market scan. Conferences, peer networks, and industry groups all contribute to a shared understanding (see chapter 11). The most efficient approach is not to try to know everything, but to know where to look and who to ask.

What matters more than knowing the market is understanding your own firm. Finding the tools is secondary; identifying the needs comes first.

START WITH THE PROBLEM, NOT THE SOLUTION

The single most common mistake in legal technology selection is starting with the tool. A partner hears about a well-capitalized legal AI tool at a conference. A client mentions a competitor's tool in passing. An associate reads about a new AI-powered research platform on LinkedIn. The conversation begins with the product, and from that point forward every discussion is framed by what that product can do rather than by what the firm broadly – and each individual practice group specifically – actually needs.

The first step in any responsible tool selection process is to map needs, not solutions. This means identifying where AI can help, where it is essential, where existing workflows can be rethought, and where the pain points are that technology might address. It means talking to lawyers about their work before talking to technology providers about their products.

This process goes by different names in different firms. Some will go on a 'listening tour'. Others conduct structured interviews with practice group leaders. Others use process mapping exercises to document how work actually flows through the firm, from matter intake to final delivery. Whatever the method, the output should ideally be a comprehensive inventory of the areas where AI could be applied, grounded in the reality of how work is done in various practice groups.

Process mapping deserves particular emphasis here because it is the foundation of not only tool selection but also the workflow automation, AI upskilling, and agentic AI applications that firms are increasingly pursuing. If you do not understand how a matter moves through a practice, how and when documents are generated and reviewed, where bottlenecks occur, and where human judgement is indispensable, you cannot make an informed decision about which tools to build or deploy to ease those pain points. In addition, if you only automate what already exists without asking whether the underlying process itself could be improved, you miss the opportunity to design something genuinely better from the ground up.

There are plenty of guides on how to process map[3] with various types of flowcharts and shapes to consider, but at its core it involves walking through every step of a task or series of tasks one by one; outlining who is responsible for that step and who they interact with; and what technology, if any, could be leveraged. When getting started, it does not matter whether you do process mapping in the 'right' way. Provided that you capture each step and can sit down at the end and review where there might be bottlenecks or issues in that process where technology could help, you will have started the journey towards identifying your problems.

PRIORITIZATION: WHAT TO SOLVE FIRST

Once you have an inventory of your pain points and potential AI applications, the next challenge is deciding where to begin. No firm has the resources to pursue everything at once. Lawyer time and attention are finite, as is IT capacity to support procurement, integration, and deployment. The question is not what could potentially be done but what should be done first.

A prioritization framework helps here.[4] The most effective frameworks assess potential applications against several dimensions: the strategic importance of the use case to the firm's direction; the size of the practice area affected; the profitability of that practice; the repeatability of the process in question; whether the solution is client-facing or a competitive differentiator; the feasibility of automation given current technology; whether a product already exists in the market; and ease of implementation.

This kind of structured ranking forces honest conversations. Not every compelling use case deserves real investment. A small practice generating modest fees can wait. But when disruption hits something central to the business, hesitation might cost more than implementing an imperfect solution. The framework creates a defensible basis for saying yes to some initiatives and no or not now to others, which is essential when partners will inevitably ask why their practice was not prioritized (see also chapter 3).

The output of this exercise should be a ranked list of problems to solve and not a ranked list of products to buy. The former allows the firm to approach the market with clear requirements whereas the latter might anchor the conversation to a specific vendor before you have a chance to determine whether that vendor is the right fit.

THE ROLE OF THE COMMITTEE

As discussed in chapter 4, an AI Committee is not optional. In the context of tool selection specifically, the committee serves as the mechanism through which competing priorities are managed and scarce resources are allocated.

The committee should be partner-led. Partners are the owners of the business. They control client relationships, they influence budgets, and they are the people whose support and sponsorship determine whether a tool succeeds or fails. If an innovation team prioritizes a third-party procurement, or builds a solution without partner buy-in, the initiative will struggle. Engagement and adoption initiatives that emanate solely from the innovation team will go unnoticed, and key performance indicators for usage will go unmet. Any initiative, process improvement, or tool must have partner buy-in and support from day one. If a partner-led committee prioritizes the initiative, the partners who participated in that decision become its champions. They were there when the decision was made. They understood why this use case was selected over others. They can advocate for it within their practices with credibility.

In conjunction with a prioritization framework, the committee also provides a defensible process for saying no. Without a representative body, decisions to deprioritize an initiative are easily challenged. A partner whose client has invested in a legal AI tool will want the firm to procure it. A partner who heard about a new contract analysis tool that addresses their exact pain point will want a pilot immediately. If the response is simply that the innovation team decided otherwise, the conversation becomes political. However, if the response is that a committee representing multiple practices evaluated the options against clear, static, and consistent criteria and made a different choice, the conversation is strategic.

CONFLICTS OF INTEREST IN TOOL SELECTION

The prevalence of investment relationships between law firm partners and legal technology companies creates a problem that the profession has not yet fully reckoned with. Partners might have clients who are investors in AI companies. They might have personal relationships with founders. In some cases, partners at a firm might sit on the board of, or hold equity in, an AI vendor that the firm is evaluating. These are not hypothetical scenarios. They are happening now, across the market, and firms need a clear-eyed approach to managing them.

Consider a firm evaluating two competing platforms. One of these platforms counts a major firm client among its investors. A senior partner, eager to maintain that client relationship, advocates strongly for that platform. The innovation team has data suggesting the other platform performs better for the firm's use cases. Without a structured evaluation process – one with transparent scoring criteria and documented reasoning – the decision risks being driven by the relationship instead of by the capabilities of the tool.

To be clear, keeping a client happy is a valuable consideration. It should probably be part of the equation above, but it should not be the deciding factor in problem prioritization or tool selection.

The question of whether firms should have mandatory disclosure requirements when partners have investment relationships with AI vendors is a live one. Existing conflict-of-interest frameworks within law firms were not designed for a world in which the tools that lawyers use every day are made by companies in which their colleagues have a financial stake. While some firms are beginning to address this, the industry as a whole has not caught up.

A structured, committee-led evaluation process, with clear criteria established before any tool demo takes place, is the strongest protection against this issue. When the scoring is transparent and the decision-making body is representative, the influence of any single relationship is diluted. That does not eliminate bias entirely, but it does make the process defensible.

THE IMPORTANCE OF KEEPING A LOG

One of the simplest but also most valuable disciplines in managing technology overload is maintaining an inventory log. Every tool that crosses the firm's radar should be recorded along with who mentioned it, when that person mentioned it, what problems it solves, what the firm's initial assessment was, where to find more information about it, and where the relationship stands.

This sounds bureaucratic, but it is not. It is sanity. When a partner emails asking about a product they heard about at a dinner, the innovation team can refer to the log and respond immediately: 'We evaluated this tool in September, here is what we found, and here is where it sits in our prioritization.' Consider it the technology analogue to a business development team tracking every touch point with a client. When the same vendor appears for the third time from three different sources, the log reveals a pattern of market interest that warrants closer attention. When a tool that was previously deprioritized releases a significant update, the log provides the context to reassess efficiently.

Whether the log is shared firm-wide or maintained internally within the innovation team is a separate question. Some firms choose to make it visible, creating a self-service resource that reduces inbound requests (using AI to talk about AI). Others keep it internal to avoid creating expectations about when tools will be evaluated. Either approach works. What does not work is having no log at all and relying on memory and email threads to manage a rapidly expanding landscape, especially if there are changes to staffing that mean the only person who remembers what happened is no longer around.

HOW TO EVALUATE AI PROVIDERS

Once the firm has identified its priority use cases and begun to shortlist potential solutions, the evaluation process begins. This is where clear requirements, established before any demo takes place, are essential.

Too many evaluations begin with an impressive demo and end with a purchase decision based on how good the demo looked.

Demos are designed to impress and to showcase the best features in ideal conditions with curated data. They are marketing rather than being a true evaluation. A rigorous evaluation requires the firm to define, in advance, what the tool must be able to do, what data it will need to process, what integrations it will require, and what performance standards it must meet.

PILOT DESIGN

Pilot design matters as much as the evaluation itself, and getting it wrong can undermine the entire exercise. The goal should be a true head-to-head comparison, as close to apples-to-apples as is possible. That means giving each tool the same tasks, the same data, and the same conditions, so that the results reflect the capability of the product rather than the circumstances of the test. If one tool gets better data or more enthusiastic participants, the comparison is meaningless before it starts.

A few things make pilots work.

- Clear engagement guidelines from day one, so participants know what they are testing, how to use the tools, and what level of engagement and feedback is expected.
- Defined success metrics established before the pilot begins, not reverse-engineered afterwards to justify a decision that has already been made.
- Regular check-ins with participants throughout the pilot period, because engagement tends to drop off after the first week, and the most valuable insights often come from sustained use, not first impressions.
- Hands-on keyboard time with the vendors, not just demos, so participants can see how the tool performs (all facets of it, in different scenarios) when they are the ones driving it.
- Access to the vendors themselves, so that questions, frustrations, and any misconceptions about features surface in real time instead of in a post-pilot survey.

It is important to keep the pilots as short as possible. This creates an engaged audience and gives you the ability to make decisions faster. No meaningful additional input will arrive after the first two or three months, other than the evolution of the product itself, which will only confuse matters.

Who participates matters as much as how the pilot is run. Select from across relevant practice groups and knowledge teams, and involve the people who will actually do the work as opposed to the loudest voices or the most political and senior people. The former will make excellent pilot participants while the latter are likely to be too busy to participate meaningfully. Make sure everyone who should be involved has the time to engage properly, because a half-committed pilot group produces half-useful data. This might mean drawing on incentives programmes, as discussed in chapter 6, or leveraging other recognition mechanisms since the pilot will take these individuals out of their daily work. Where possible, allow participants to use the tools on live matters, real documents, and real deals, not curated test sets. This is where performance differences emerge.

Structured data collection at every stage is essential. The data needs to be both quantitative (usage rates, task completion times, accuracy) and qualitative (what was intuitive, what felt clunky, what was missing). Build in regular opportunities for feedback – formal and informal – and make sure your methods of collection are clean enough that you can genuinely compare the products side by side when the pilot ends. If you have a large enough team, it also helps to ensure that the people evaluating the pilot results are not the same people who selected the tools being piloted. Preferences in law firms are shaped by relationships, by which partner championed which product, by which vendor made the better pitch. Without separation between selection and evaluation, those preferences can colour the interpretation of the data. The goal is to create conditions where the tool's performance speaks for itself rather than being filtered through the preferences and politics of the firm.

PRACTICE AREA EXPERTISE

A recurring lesson from evaluations is that you cannot assess a legal AI tool in the abstract. A tool that works brilliantly for corporate M&A due diligence may be mediocre at best for disputes research or eDiscovery, and a platform that excels at contract review might fall short when it comes to regulatory advice. The nuances of each practice area, the types of documents, the nature of the analysis, and the jurisdictional requirements mean that meaningful evaluation requires input from lawyers who actually do the work.

Innovation teams that try to evaluate tools on their own, without bringing in subject matter experts from the relevant practices and adjacent business services teams, risk making selections that look good on paper but fail in production. The lawyers know what a good output looks like, and they know the edge cases. They can spot when a tool is giving confident but incorrect answers in their domain.

REFERENCE CHECKS AND PEER CONVERSATIONS

Vendor marketing materials are useful but insufficient. The most valuable evaluations include conversations with peers, i.e. firms of similar size, in similar markets, with similar practice mixes, who have deployed the tool in production. These conversations reveal what the vendor may not tell you, such as how long implementation actually took, what broke during deployment (or continues to break), how responsive post-sales support was and for how long, and whether the tool delivered on its promises once the initial excitement faded.

Vendors should be asked to provide references, and firms should make the time to follow up on them. Investing in a thirty-minute call with a peer who has lived with the tool for six months is worth more than hours of vendor presentations.

BENCHMARKING AND THE MOVING TARGET PROBLEM

Benchmarking AI tools presents a challenge that did not exist with previous generations of legal technology. The tools change constantly. A benchmark conducted in January might be irrelevant by March, not because the evaluation was flawed but because the underlying models, features, and integrations have changed.

In the early days of AI in the profession, firms and in-house teams spent significant time comparing tools side by side. Which model produced more accurate contract summaries? Which was better at legal research? These comparisons were valuable at the time, but the shift to multimodel architectures and the speed of updates has made model-level benchmarking less relevant for most firms. Many of the leading legal AI platforms now route queries to different models depending on the task, selecting the most appropriate model for the specific request. The relevant question has shifted from which model is best to which platform uses its models most effectively for legal work.

What is of more value now is holistic external benchmarking. Industry analysts, legal technology publications, and community resources provide ongoing data on tool performance. These are more sustainable than internal benchmarking exercises that quickly go stale, though they should be supplemented with the firm's own evaluation if a shortlisted tool is being seriously considered.

Ultimately, the underlying tension is real, since firms want certainty in a market that cannot provide it. The best response is not to seek certainty but to build an evaluation process that is repeatable. If a tool is evaluated rigorously today and the evaluation becomes outdated in six months, then, if done properly, the framework for re-evaluation already exists. The discipline of the process matters more than the permanence of any individual result.

ONE PLATFORM OR MANY TOOLS?

One of the most consequential decisions a firm will make is whether to pursue a singular platform strategy or a portfolio of point solutions. The answer depends on the firm's size, its risk appetite, its practice mix, and its philosophy when it comes to technology management.

Platforms such as Harvey and Legora have positioned themselves as the operating system of the law firm. They offer a single environment for multiple use cases (drafting; research; contract review; and, increasingly, agentic workflows). The appeal of this approach is obvious: one tool means one training programme, one integration, one vendor relationship, one set of data governance requirements. For firm leadership, a platform operating system simplifies management and creates a coherent narrative about the firm's technology strategy. This mechanism also helps with adoption, since lawyers remember where to find the tool and they become familiar with its interface.

But the appeal of a singular platform can obscure its limitations. No platform does everything equally well. Disputes teams will not route all of their eDiscovery work through a general-purpose AI tool if, for example, the firm also uses Relativity or Everlaw, built for that purpose. Real estate practices might find that a specialized tool such as Orbital, with its connections to land registries and title databases, outperforms a general platform for property due diligence. Legal research has specific demands that might not be well served by a tool whose primary strength lies in document drafting and that has no true proprietary set of underlying data to support legal research.

Both firm leadership and vendors have strong incentives to push every use case into the primary platform. Leadership wants to maximize the return on a significant investment. Vendors want to demonstrate breadth and deepen their integration. But the innovation team, the adjacent business services teams, the knowledge lawyers, and the practice-embedded specialists who understand the nuances of each area of work play a critical role in pushing back. Their job is to know where the workbench tool's capabilities end and where point solutions remain necessary. Without that expertise, firms risk deploying tools beyond their effective range, creating frustration among lawyers and potentially compromising the quality of output.

There is a broader point here that goes beyond any individual procurement decision. Most firms are now operating with a mix of general-purpose platforms, specialist point solutions, copilots embedded in productivity suites, and an expanding collection of internally built tools and workflows. While each might be individually justified, taken together they create an environment that can be genuinely confusing for the lawyers expected to use them. Which tool do I use for this task? Where does my work get saved? Which system has the most current version of this document? Does the output from one tool transfer cleanly into another?

This is not a training problem, it is a design problem, and it is becoming a strategic issue in its own right. Adoption depends on the experience being coherent. A lawyer who has to think about which tool to use before starting a task is a lawyer who will default to doing things the old way. Agents, MCP, and the move by foundation model companies such as Anthropic to build product layers on top of their own models will go some way towards mitigating this issue by providing a single interface connected to multiple solutions,[5] but they are not a magic wand. The firms that solve this – whether through thoughtful integration, clear internal guidance, or simply by being disciplined about how many tools they allow into the environment at any one time – will see higher and more sustained adoption than those that treat each tool as a standalone decision. The question is not just which tools to select but how those tools fit together as a working environment that lawyers can navigate without friction.

PREFERRED, PERMITTED, PROHIBITED

The most practical framework for managing the tension between platform and point solutions is to leverage the previously discussed AI policy to help with adoption by classifying tools into three categories for each use case: preferred, permitted, and prohibited.

Preferred is the firm's recommended tool for a given use case. It has been fully evaluated, is supported by the innovation team, and has been approved by risk and data governance. Training is available and support is in place.

Permitted tools have been evaluated and are approved for use, but they are not the firm's first choice. They might serve specific needs that the preferred tool does not cover, or they might be the tool of choice for a particular practice group with a strong reason for divergence. A real estate team using Orbital Copilot for property due diligence alongside a general platform such as Harvey or Legora is a good example. While the general platform might be the firm's preferred tool for most AI-assisted work, Orbital is permitted, and in fact better suited, for this specific use case.

Prohibited tools are not approved for the use case. That does not mean they are bad tools. It means that they have not been evaluated for this specific purpose, that they do not meet the firm's data governance requirements, that they are more expensive to use, or that they are simply the wrong tool for the job.

This classification should be maintained as a living appendix to the firm's AI policy, updated as tools are evaluated and as capabilities change. It provides clear guidance to lawyers who want to know what they should use, and it provides a defensible basis for the innovation team when they need to redirect a practice group away from an inappropriate tool. Perhaps most importantly, it prevents the natural tendency, common in firms that have made a significant investment in a single platform, for leadership and vendor alike to push every use case into the preferred tool, regardless of whether it is actually a good fit.

BUILD, BUY, OR RENT

As discussed briefly in chapter 4, the traditional technology debate in law firms was build versus buy. Do you develop a bespoke solution in-house or purchase a commercial product? AI has introduced a third concept that might increasingly become the default: renting.

Renting, in the sense of treating AI tooling as modular and replaceable rather than deeply embedded, allows firms to invest lightly and avoid becoming too attached to any single platform. The AI landscape is evolving so rapidly that any tool selected today may be superseded within eighteen months. Firms that invest heavily in deep integration with a single vendor risk being locked in when a better option emerges. Firms that treat their AI tools as interchangeable components, connected to firm infrastructure but not embedded so deeply that they cannot be swapped out, retain the flexibility to adapt.

Think of it the way you think about renting an apartment. You get the benefit of living there, you learn the neighbourhood, you figure out what you actually need, and if something better comes along or the landlord raises the rent beyond what the place is worth, you can move. You have not poured your savings into a renovation you cannot take with you. In a market this volatile, that flexibility is a strategic advantage, not a compromise.

That does not mean firms should avoid investment. It means they should invest strategically, keeping their core infrastructure – particularly document management systems and enterprise search functionalities – as the stable foundation and treating AI tools as the components that sit on top. The foundation should be solid and enduring, but the component parts should be replaceable.

The rise of general-purpose development tools complicates this picture further. When a technically capable lawyer or a small internal team can prototype a workflow in an evening using tools such as Claude Code, Codex, or Lovable, the question of build versus buy becomes less about institutional capability and more about individual initiative. This is explored in detail in chapter 9 but it warrants mention here because it affects how firms think about procurement. If lawyers are building their own tools, the procurement function must account for what is being built internally, not simply what is available from third parties.

THE PROCUREMENT PROCESS

Once a tool has been selected, the procurement process determines whether the firm gets value from its investment. Procurement is not simply about price, it is about ensuring that the vendor relationship supports the firm's needs over the lifetime of the engagement, not just at the point of sale.

The questions a firm should ask during procurement reflect the realities of working with rapidly evolving AI tools. What does the implementation process look like and who is responsible for configuration? How does this tool integrate with your ecosystem and who has the expertise and relationships to secure those integrations? How long does it take and what resources does the firm need to provide? Implementation is where many tools fail. A product that looks excellent in a demo or even a pilot can struggle in production if the firm's data, systems, and workflows do not align with assumptions and promises.

Post-sales support is consistently cited by firms as one of the most important, and most uneven, aspects of vendor relationships. The enthusiasm that vendors show during the sales process does not always survive the transition to an established account. Firms should ask about dedicated customer success managers, escalation paths, and ongoing engagement models before signing any contract.

Training support should be a partnership, not an afterthought. As discussed in chapter 6, training is a continuous process, and vendors that provide strong, ongoing training support significantly improve adoption rates. The vendor should be invested in the firm's success with the product, not simply in closing the sale.

THE UPDATE PROBLEM

The pace of change in AI tools poses a procurement challenge that has no real precedent in legal technology. When a vendor changes its underlying model, switches a third-party integration, or adds a new feature, the firm's security and governance teams might need to reassess. But these changes can happen on timescales that are incompatible with traditional procurement review cycles.

This problem is not a theoretical one. Firms have encountered situations where a vendor switched its web search provider without advance notice, creating a potential security concern that the firm's risk team had not evaluated. Other firms have found that new features appeared in the product, sometimes advertised directly to end users through in-app notifications or pop-ups, before the firm's innovation team had been informed let alone had the chance to assess whether those features were appropriate for the firm's use.

The communication problem runs in multiple directions. Vendors announce capabilities on LinkedIn and social media as a marketing exercise, and partners and associates see those announcements before the innovation team has been briefed or before there is any real information on which to be briefed. The innovation team then fields questions about features it cannot yet evaluate or has not yet evaluated, creating a reactive posture that undermines the careful, structured approach described throughout this chapter.

Managing this requires a combination of contractual provisions – specifically the right to be notified of material changes before they take effect – and operational discipline. One effective approach is to curate vendor update communications into a regular digest for the relevant stakeholders, filtering out the noise and highlighting changes that actually matter to the firm's use of the tool. This takes time and expertise but it prevents the alternative of lawyers being blindsided by changes they do not understand or of innovation teams spending their days responding to partner emails about features they have not had time to assess. There are multiple ways to solve this problem, but it is certainly something to be aware of and stay on top of when vendors are competing with each other at lightning speed, and all of their customers have different features enabled, or release new product features at different cadences to end-users.

SANDBOX ENVIRONMENTS

In the past, when software was installed on premises, vendors needed IT teams within organizations to release new updates, and rigorous testing within the organization's development environment was required. The switch to cloud offerings removed the IT control over the process, and yet testing features in a sandbox environment before they reach production remains essential. Vendors should provide sandbox or staging environments in which the firm can evaluate new features, test configurations, and identify issues before they affect the live system. This is standard practice in enterprise software but it is not always available or well supported in the legal AI market. Firms should make sandbox access a requirement during procurement, not an afterthought.

The sandbox question ties into a broader point about the maturity of the legal AI vendor ecosystem. Many of these companies are young, venture-backed, and moving fast. That speed is part of their appeal, but it also means that the enterprise-grade infrastructure that large law firms expect – staging environments, change management protocols, advance notification of updates – is not always in place. Firms should be direct about these expectations during the procurement process. If a vendor cannot provide a sandbox, that is information worth having before the contract is signed, not after.

SECURITY AND DATA GOVERNANCE IN PROCUREMENT

Security and data governance, explored more fully in chapter 8, are a critical part of the procurement conversation and deserve a brief mention here. Where is data stored? Who has access? What third-party services does the product use? How are security changes communicated? These questions should be addressed before signing up to a new tool.

The profession's evolving comfort with AI tools follows a familiar pattern. A decade ago some courts prohibited the use of machine learning technology to expedite document review, but today that is the standard. Similarly, data rooms were once considered risky. The idea of putting confidential deal documents on a third-party server, accessible via the internet, met with significant resistance. Now data rooms are a trusted infrastructure, not because the risks have disappeared but because clients and firms have become comfortable with them over time and because the industry has built standards and practices around their use. AI tools are on a similar trajectory. The risks are real but they are manageable, and the firms that figure out how to manage them now will be better positioned than those that wait for certainty that may never arrive.

One irony is worth noting because it speaks to the familiar pattern noted above. Firms currently invest significant effort in ensuring their AI tools respect the ethical walls and matter boundaries enforced by their document management systems, mapping folders, workspaces, and matter numbers to ensure that confidential information does not cross boundaries. And then, once inside some of these AI platforms, users can share projects and workspaces with anyone at the firm. The effort spent on gates in front of the house is undermined by open windows when you get inside. This is a solvable problem but it requires firms to look at the full lifecycle of data within these tools, not just at the point of ingestion.

A related question is whether law firms that build and deploy their own tools, particularly those that serve clients directly, should be held to the same security and compliance standards as the vendors they procure from. Some firms have already obtained SOC 2 Type II and ISO 27001 certification for their own technology operations to showcase their commitment to cybersecurity.[6] Whether this becomes an industry standard remains to be seen, but as the line between law firm and technology provider continues to blur, the issue will only become more pressing. This will be explored further in chapter 9.

MANAGING TECH OVERLOAD

The overload problem is not just about the number of tools available, it is about the cognitive and organizational burden of keeping pace with a market that moves faster than any firm's ability to evaluate it.

Several practical disciplines help manage this burden. First, do not try to know everything. Rely on external resources, directories, peer networks, and consultancies for market awareness (see chapter 11). Focus internal resources on deep evaluation of shortlisted tools for your priority use cases.

Second, centralize the intake process. Every request for a new tool or capability, whether it comes from a partner, a client, or an associate who saw something online, should flow through a single point of coordination. This prevents duplication, ensures visibility, and allows the innovation team to see patterns in demand.

Third, maintain the log. As described earlier, a continuously maintained inventory of tools evaluated, in progress, and rejected provides institutional memory that prevents re-evaluation of tools that have already been assessed.

Fourth, communicate decisions, not just tools. When a tool is selected, deprioritized, or rejected, communicate the reasoning to the relevant stakeholders. This builds trust in the process and reduces the tendency for individuals to pursue their own technology agendas outside of the established framework.

And finally, accept imperfection. No evaluation will be definitive. No selection will be permanent. The goal is not to find the perfect tool but to find the right tool for right now, with a process in place to reassess as the market evolves. Firms expecting certainty will wait forever. The firms that move, with discipline and with process, will be the ones that learn fastest and adapt most effectively.

LOOKING AHEAD

Tool selection does not exist in isolation. Once a tool has been selected and procured, the questions shift to how to address the baseline compliance requirements that any tool must meet before it is deployed; how to ensure data security; how to govern a tool's use; and how to manage the ongoing relationship with the vendor.

It also connects backwards, to the team structures and skills discussed in chapter 4, to the data foundations discussed in chapter 5, and to the training and adoption strategies discussed in chapter 6. Rather than being a standalone exercise, tool selection is one step in a continuous process of assessment, deployment, monitoring, and adaptation.

The firms and legal teams that navigate this well will be those that invest in processes rather than in any single product. Products will come and go (see chapter 9), but the discipline of knowing what you need, evaluating it rigorously, deploying it thoughtfully, and monitoring it continuously is what separates firms that are genuinely transforming their practice from those that are simply buying software and hoping for the best.

IN PRACTICE

In a Sentence

To survive the pace of change and innovation in the legal AI market, invest in the processes for knowing what is needed, not in tracking any single product.

What to Remember

- Do not start with a tool. Map your needs first so you understand the 'why' that the tools are solving.
- Prioritization is not optional. Assess potential applications across strategic importance, practice size and profitability, process repeatability, and implementation feasibility so that you can rank the problems to solve first.
- An AI Committee turns contentious decisions into defensible ones. When a firm says no to a partner's tool of choice, it matters whether the reason is 'your preference lost' or 'a representative committee applied static criteria'.
- 'Preferred, permitted, and prohibited' is a classification that scales. It tells lawyers which tool to use for what, which tools are allowed outside the main platform, and which tools are off limits, so that decisions do not have to be constantly debated.
- Rent rather than buy. Treat AI tools as modular components that can be swapped out, not infrastructure to embed. Keep the core (document management, search, identity) stable and let the AI layer on top stay light. Other than a few main systems you have to commit to, the market moves too fast to lock in.

What to Do with This

- Conduct process mapping before you talk to vendors. Walk through each task one step at a time, documenting who is responsible, where the handoffs are, and where a tool could genuinely help.
- Keep an inventory log of every tool that crosses your organization's radar, with the date, who raised it, the problems it solves, your assessment, and where the relationship stands. The log is how you spot patterns, avoid repeat evaluations, and reassess tools that looked immature a quarter ago.
- Define success criteria before the demo not after the pilot. Specify what the tool must do, what data it will process, what integrations it needs, and what success looks like.

Questions to Sit With

» Who in your organization has the credibility to say no to a tool rather than deflecting, and is that role formalized or informal?

» If a vendor's model changes materially next quarter, who notices, who decides what to do about it, and how do you communicate the decision across the firm?

» Are there use cases where a specialized point solution would outperform your preferred general AI platform, and are you willing to defend that to leadership who would rather consolidate most, if not all, practice group requests into a single vendor offering?

CHAPTER 8

Risk, Privacy, and Data Governance

We should note at the outset of this chapter that we are not providing legal advice. The regulatory landscape, the case law, and the technology are all evolving too quickly for any single source to serve as definitive guidance. What follows is designed to help you think through the risks, understand the mitigations that are available today, and build a framework for responsible adoption. Readers should consult qualified counsel in their own jurisdictions for advice on specific situations.

Before addressing any specific risk, this chapter begins with a (potentially provocative) framework for thinking through risk. The greatest risk facing the legal profession is not a data breach, a hallucination, or a regulatory penalty. Rather, during this time of immense change, the biggest risk is inaction, lack of experimentation, and a failure to be curious.

Firms and in-house teams that do not learn how to operate in this new environment will find themselves irrelevant for an increasing share of the work that is coming. Every risk discussed in this chapter is real, and each must be taken seriously. But every one of them can be mitigated through education, planning, and the right infrastructure and guardrails. The risk of standing still cannot be effectively mitigated.

The legal profession has a well-documented bias toward the status quo and risk aversion.[1] Lawyers are trained to identify risk, and they are rewarded for caution. When confronted with a technology that generates different answers to the same question; that changes and evolves, month to month; and that operates in ways that resist precise explanation, the instinct of many lawyers is to wait. Wait for the rules to settle. Wait for the market to stabilize. Wait for someone else to go first.

That instinct, however rational it might feel, is becoming the most expensive decision a lawyer can make. The firms that are moving now are building their capabilities, training their people, and learning through practice what does and does not work for their use cases and workflow. The firms that are waiting are falling behind in ways that will become increasingly difficult to reverse.

Imagine what it will be like if, in a few years' time, all business is conducted in a language you do not speak. You have the opportunity now to start learning. Those who wait may find that by the time they begin, everyone else is already fluent.

WHAT KEEPS PEOPLE PARALYZED

Before turning to specific risks, it is worth naming the broader uncertainties that create paralysis. Understanding why people hesitate is essential to designing frameworks that help them move forward.

Probabilistic Decision Making

The first uncertainty is the nature of the technology itself. Large language models are probabilistic. If you ask the same question twice, you may get different answers, and for a profession built on precision, predictability, and the ability to cite authority, this is deeply uncomfortable. Lawyers want certainty and that is what their clients expect.

The Pace of Change

The second uncertainty is the pace of market change. The tools available today may not be the tools that will be dominant in six months' time, and even if they are they might have changed significantly. Firms do not know which products will survive or what the competitive landscape will look like in two years. It is a lot of work to test, procure, and implement new technology, particularly within law firms where the risk landscape is more cautious. This creates a natural reluctance to commit. As discussed in chapters 7 and 9, the tool selection landscape is evolving at a speed that has no precedent in the profession, and this instability compounds the hesitation many lawyers, and the technology teams supporting them, already feel.

The Business Model

The third uncertainty is the business model. As discussed in chapter 3, most firms still operate on a billable hour model that rewards effort rather than efficiency, and many worry (correctly) that in the current traditional firm framework, a tool that makes work faster will also make it less profitable.

Regulatory Environment

The fourth uncertainty is the regulatory environment. Courts, bar associations, and ethics committees are issuing guidance and rulings regularly. In early 2026 the competing decisions in *United States v. Heppner*[2] and *Warner v. Gilbarco, Inc.*[3] on AI and privilege are only the most prominent examples.[4] Lawyers worry that what they do today may be judged differently tomorrow. In the United Kingdom, the Solicitors Regulation Authority was slow to introduce any specific regulatory guidance, and those waiting for guidance on how to proceed have found themselves left behind.

Competence Levels

The fifth uncertainty is competence itself. Lawyers are entering unfamiliar territory. They are not data scientists and nor are they software engineers (see, however, chapter 9). The anxiety of operating outside one's expertise is real, and it is compounded by a professional culture that equates competence with certainty. Lawyers are used to being the smartest person in the room and they can therefore be reluctant to discuss a topic that they do not understand.

Moving Ahead

None of these uncertainties is trivial, but taken together they create a bias towards the status quo that is itself the most significant risk.

For each category of risk that we discuss below, the concern is identified, there is an explanation of why it matters, and practical approaches for managing it are offered. The goal is not to eliminate risk, which is impossible, but to make it manageable so that it does not become a reason to do nothing.

WHERE THE RISKS ARE AND HOW TO MANAGE THEM

Competence and Responsibility

ABA Model Rule 1.1 requires lawyers to provide competent representation, which includes keeping abreast of changes in the law and its practice, including the benefits and risks associated with relevant technology.[5] Likewise, the Solicitors Regulation Authority (SRA) Code of Conduct for Solicitors contains similar competency requirements under paragraphs 3.2, 3.3, and 3.6.[6] In the context of AI these obligations have taken on new and evolving weight. Sufficient competence really requires familiarity with two parallel tracks. The first relates to the tools the firm has procured and deployed, i.e. understanding what they can do, what their limitations are, and how to use them effectively. The second, which is equally important, relates to the broader landscape of AI capabilities as they exist outside the firm. Law firms will always lag behind the frontier of what is technically possible. Their procurement cycles, security reviews, and governance processes ensure that the tools available to lawyers inside the firm are months or even years behind what is available on the open market. A lawyer who only understands what the firm's tools can do is not fully competent. A competent lawyer must also understand what the technology is capable of more broadly, even if the firm has not yet deployed those capabilities.

The practical risk of non-compliance with the ABA's Rule 1.1 and the SRA's Code of Conduct is professional negligence. Many lawyers have not been upskilled on when or how to use AI, or they misuse the technology by failing to verify outputs, using AI for tasks it is not suited to, or they over-rely on AI-generated analysis without applying professional judgement. Rather than being simply an adoption problem, insufficient training presents a professional liability. The 2026 SKILLS survey shows that nearly 57% of firms report that more than half their lawyers have completed baseline AI training.[7] However, this also means that 43% of firms have trained fewer than half of their lawyers, highlighting how uneven AI training adoption remains across the industry.

Continuing legal education must evolve to include AI competence as a core component, not an optional supplement. The distinction between knowing how to use a tool and knowing when not to use it is one that training programmes must address head-on. A lawyer who can operate an AI system fluently but cannot recognize when it is producing unreliable outputs is not a competent user of the technology. Competence in AI, like competence in law, requires judgement, and judgement requires experience that can only be built through guided, supervised practice.

Beyond this basic competence framework, AI introduces risks that go to the quality and integrity of the work itself. Identifying bias in outputs is the most legally consequential emerging risk here. AI systems trained on historical data will reflect the biases present in that data. In practice areas where bias has direct consequences, such as employment law, criminal justice, immigration, and lending, the risk is acute. Emerging regulations in several jurisdictions require organizations to assess and address bias in AI systems used for decision-making.[8] Lawyers who use AI outputs without understanding or checking for bias risk producing work-product that is not only inaccurate but actively harmful. The severity of this risk varies by practice area, and firms should assess where bias poses the greatest threat to the quality of their work and direct their attention there first. Training should include simulated scenarios where lawyers encounter biased or unreliable AI outputs and it must identify the problems before acting on them.

Finally, environmental responsibility is an emerging consideration. AI systems consume significant computational resources, and some organizations have begun to consider energy consumption as part of their responsible AI frameworks.[9] This extends to law firms. While this has not emerged as the most pressing business risk in the current landscape, it remains important and reflects a broader expectation that firms will use AI thoughtfully, not wastefully. Firms that incorporate energy consumption into their AI use policies send a signal, both internally and to clients, that their approach to AI is considered rather than indiscriminate.

Client Confidentiality

Client confidentiality sits at the intersection of a lawyer's ethical duties and the firm's obligations under data protection and data privacy law. The ethical duty that a lawyer must not disclose client information without informed consent is well understood, but the data protection dimension adds further layers of obligation. Regulations such as the General Data Protection Regulation (GDPR) and the California Consumer Privacy Act (CCPA) impose specific requirements on how personal data is collected, stored, processed, and transferred, and AI tools that ingest client materials may trigger all of these requirements. A firm that sends client data to an external AI system without understanding the data processing implications is not only risking a breach of confidentiality, it may also be in breach of its data protection obligations.

The risk takes several forms. Some AI systems train on user inputs, and a lawyer who enters client information into such a system may be contributing that information to a dataset that influences future outputs for other users. Also, shareable links and collaborative features can expose information beyond its intended audience. There is a documented instance of Google indexing shareable ChatGPT links, meaning that conversations a user believed were private became searchable on the open web.[10] Finally, the proliferation of AI-powered tools that request broad system access, such as certain agent-based applications, creates the risk that a lawyer grants an AI system access to files and systems far beyond what was intended. This last category is evolving rapidly at the time of writing. When a user downloads agent-based tools to their computers without a full understanding of what they are or what they do, they may expose and grant access to their terminal, their file system, and their (i.e. the firm's) network. The democratization of AI agents has outpaced most lawyers' understanding of what they are actually consenting to when they install and authorize these tools. Where personal data is involved, this kind of uncontrolled access might also raise data privacy concerns, particularly in jurisdictions with strict rules on cross-border data transfers.

The mitigations fall under three headings. First, *education*. Lawyers must understand how the tools they use handle data, what is stored, what is shared, what is used for model training, and what is excluded. This extends to understanding data protection measures, such as where the data is processed, whether appropriate data processing agreements are in place, and whether the firm's use of the tool complies with applicable privacy regulations.

Second, *prevention*. Firms can deploy technical safeguards that monitor and control what data leaves the firm's environment. Some firms block document uploads to web search features within their AI tools, accepting a reduction in functionality in exchange for a hard guarantee that no client documents are sent to external search providers. Others deploy data loss prevention tools purpose-built for AI workflows. There are governance tools, for example, which provide an anonymization layer, scrubbing identifying information before data is sent to external AI systems and then replacing it on the way back. This means that the lawyer sees real names but the AI system never does.

Third, *creating safe alternatives* with on-premises or private-cloud deployments of local language models allows lawyers to experiment freely within an environment where no data gets through the firm's firewall. If the firm provides a safe space in which lawyers can use AI without risk of leakage, the temptation to use unsanctioned external tools diminishes (see also 'Governing the Build: Frameworks, Not Prohibition' in chapter 9). These safe alternatives also simplify data protection compliance, since data that never leaves the firm's infrastructure does not trigger cross-border transfer restrictions.

Privilege

There is an emerging, if limited, risk that communications between lawyer and client lose their protected status when routed through an AI system. This is distinct from confidentiality. While confidentiality addresses the risk of data leakage, privilege addresses the risk of waiver – and the consequences of waiver can be catastrophic in litigation. Privilege, once lost, might not be recoverable.

As mentioned earlier, as of early 2026 two federal court decisions have begun to define this area of law in the United States, and they point in different directions. In *United States v. Heppner*,[11] Judge Rakoff held that documents generated by a criminal defendant using a publicly available AI tool were not privileged and did not qualify as protected work product. The court reasoned that the defendant had not acted at counsel's direction and had been informed that his data might be disclosed to third parties; under those circumstances, neither attorney–client privilege nor the work-product doctrine applied. Alternatively, in *Warner v. Gilbarco, Inc.*,[12] Magistrate Judge Patti reached the opposite conclusion, holding that a *pro se* civil litigant's ChatGPT queries and the AI's responses were protected by the work-product doctrine. The court found that the materials reflected the plaintiff's mental impressions prepared in anticipation of litigation, and that under Sixth Circuit law, disclosing information to ChatGPT did not constitute a waiver because waiver requires disclosure to an adversary or in a manner likely to reach an adversary's hands.

In England and Wales, the first instance of a court commenting on this issue arose in *Munir v Secretary of State for the Home Department*.[13] In the case, the Upper Tribunal (Immigration and Asylum Chamber) stated that uploading client information to open-source AI tools such as ChatGPT placed information 'in the public domain, and thus … breach[es] client confidentiality and waives legal privilege', which may lead to the lawyers involved being referred to the Solicitors Regulation Authority.

These three decisions, issued in the same month, illustrate how unsettled this area of law remains. The critical variables appear to be the context in which the AI tool is used, whether counsel directed the use, the terms of service governing the platform, and whether the jurisdiction treats disclosure to an AI system as disclosure to a third party. Practitioners should expect this landscape to shift as more courts weigh in.

The practical takeaway, regardless of which line of reasoning prevails, is that tools that have been vetted and procured by the firm, that operate under appropriate data processing agreements, and that maintain confidentiality protections present a far lower privilege risk than consumer-grade AI tools used without safeguards. The current mitigations mirror those for confidentiality. First, education to ensure lawyers understand the distinction between confidentiality and privilege, and why the privilege risk demands particular care. Second, prevention to block or monitor use of unapproved tools for any work touching privileged material. And third, safe alternatives that provide the capability lawyers need within a protected environment where no data leaves the firm's control.

Talking to Clients about AI

Clients are increasingly setting expectations about AI use through outside counsel guidelines (OCGs), and firms must navigate these restrictions without undermining trust or losing the benefits of the technology. The 2026 SKILLS community survey data[14] shows that a significant proportion of clients have some form of restriction in place, so the question is not whether to address this, but how.

In practice, these restrictions are not blanket bans but invitations to conversation. The most sophisticated clients – those who understand AI well enough to specify restrictions – are often the most receptive to its use when the firm demonstrates competence and a responsible approach. These clients know what and how to restrict, and why, and if the firm can match that sophistication, the conversation shifts from prohibition to collaboration. The clients who issue no guidance at all might, paradoxically, be harder to engage on the topic, precisely because they have not yet thought through the implications. The experience of firms that have engaged proactively with their most restrictive clients may be instructive, as those clients, once satisfied that the firm understands the technology and has appropriate safeguards in place, often become the most enthusiastic advocates for AI-assisted work, and in some cases they begin to demand it.

The mitigations for this issue are relational and organizational. Primarily, partners must be educated so they understand the technology well enough to speak about it credibly. A partner who cannot explain how the firm's AI tools handle data will not inspire confidence, no matter how good the firm's governance framework is.

In addition, there should be proactive client conversations led by relationship partners where AI uses are discussed with clients. Relationship partners should explain the firm's strategy, the tools in use, the safeguards in place, and the benefits the client will receive.

Finally, some firms have found that having innovation team members speak directly with clients alongside partners about technology strategy builds confidence more effectively than having partners relay the information second hand. The partner provides the relationship context while the innovation professional provides the additional technical credibility. Neither is as persuasive alone as they are together. The roles and responsibilities of innovation teams in supporting client conversations are discussed in chapter 4.

The business model question lurks behind every client conversation about AI. If the firm is using AI to work more efficiently, the client will eventually ask why they are paying the same amount. The answer is that AI does not necessarily reduce the total cost of legal work. Instead, it changes the nature of that work: less time spent on routine tasks and more on higher-value analysis, and often a more thorough and rigorous work product.

The Billable Hour and the Jevons Paradox

The concern regarding the billable hour misunderstands what actually happens when lawyers gain capacity from increased efficiency. Economists call it the Jevons paradox; that is, when a resource becomes more efficient to use, people use more of it, not less (see chapter 3). A lawyer who finishes a task in two hours instead of six does not sit idle for four hours. That lawyer takes on more work, does deeper analysis, or catches issues that would previously have gone unreviewed. Consider a concrete example of a lawyer who uses AI to review a draft contract and returns a thirty-six-page markup where a manual review might have produced eight pages. The work is more thorough, but it also generates more work for the other side to address. Instead of decreasing, the total volume of legal activity around the transaction has increased, and the quality is higher. The real effect of AI is not always that firms do the same work faster. It is that firms can do more work, and better work, in the same amount of time.

For in-house teams, the same can apply. In a confidential conversation with one of the authors, a general counsel discussed how a redundancy procedure at their organization had led to more work rather than less. The issue for the business was that in previous redundancy situations, only a small number of employees affected by the redundancy raised queries that had to be dealt with by the legal team. Now that everyone has access to AI, though, the latest redundancy round resulted in almost every single affected employee asking a raft of insightful questions. This ultimately led to the in-house team having to instruct a panel firm instead of handling it themselves, as they would have done in the past.

Internal Governance: The AI Use Policy

Every risk discussed in this chapter – competence and responsibility, client confidentiality, data protection, data privacy, attorney–client privilege, and the management of client expectations – converges on a single practical requirement: the firm must establish a clear, comprehensive AI use policy. Internal governance is not a separate risk category. It is the mechanism by which all other risks are managed. A firm without a coherent AI use policy is a firm in which each of the risks discussed above is being handled in an ad hoc and inconsistent way, if indeed they are being handled at all.

An effective AI use policy does more than list prohibitions. It creates clearly defined spaces where lawyers know exactly what they can do, with what tools, and under what conditions. The policy should specify, for each use case, the firm's preferred tool, any permitted alternatives, and what is prohibited. This framework, which we discussed in detail in chapter 7 as the preferred/permitted/prohibited classification, is the operational expression of the firm's risk management strategy.

A critical takeaway here is that an AI use policy should be designed to drive adoption, not to drive people away. A policy that only says no, listing only prohibitions without corresponding permissions, will create the conditions for shadow AI. Lawyers who are told they cannot use AI without being given a clear, supported, and easy path to approved use will find their own way. They will use personal accounts on consumer AI tools. They will download applications without understanding the access they are granting. They will do what lawyers have always done when confronted with bureaucratic obstacles to getting work done: they will work around them. The policy must make compliance easier than non-compliance.

The general counsel or risk function should have a meaningful role in both the development and ongoing oversight of the policy, as discussed in the context of the AI Committee in chapter 4. This provides not only governance rigour but also a practical benefit, because when the risk function has been involved in approving a tool or use case, it is able to defend that decision if challenged. A firm that has the general counsel's sign-off on its AI deployment is in a fundamentally different position from one where the innovation team made the decision without risk input. The former can point to a process. The latter is exposed.

The policy itself should be treated as a living document. The pace of change in AI tools and the regulatory landscape means that a policy written in January may need revision by June. Firms should build in a regular review cycle, ideally aligned with the cadence of their AI Committee meetings, and they should designate clear ownership of the policy so that updates happen promptly rather than languishing in drafting limbo. A stale AI use policy is worse than no policy at all because it creates the illusion of governance without the substance. Equally important, the policy must be communicated in terms that lawyers can act on. A ten-page document full of caveats and conditions is unlikely to change behaviour. A clear, short summary that says 'here is what you can do, here is where you do it, and here is what you must not do' is far more likely to be read, understood, and followed.

LOOKING AHEAD

Risk management in the context of AI is not a static exercise. The tools change, the regulatory landscape evolves, and the profession's understanding of appropriate use deepens over time. The framework set out in this chapter is designed to be an adaptable structure for thinking about risk that can accommodate new risks as they emerge.

What should be clear by now is that the risks are real but manageable, and that the cost of inaction exceeds the cost of any individual risk discussed above. The organizations that build serious governance frameworks, invest in education, and create safe environments for experimentation will not eliminate risk, but they will be able to manage it, and that is all any responsible organization can do. Those that use risk as a reason to wait will find, in time, that they have traded a manageable set of risks for an existential one.

The mitigation tactics for the risks discussed in this chapter are largely the same: education, prevention, safe alternatives. These are natural extensions of the governance frameworks that responsible firms already have in place for other areas of practice. The difference is that AI moves faster than any previous technology, and the governance frameworks must be designed to keep pace.

The next chapter turns to a phenomenon that sits at the intersection of innovation and risk: the rise of vibe coding and shadow AI, where lawyers are building their own tools and using

AI outside of official channels. This creates both opportunity and new categories of risk that require their own response.

IN PRACTICE

In a Sentence

Inaction is the risk that lawyers should be most worried about, because every other risk is manageable through education, prevention, and safe alternatives.

What to Remember

» Regulatory requirements surrounding lawyer competence now extend to the broader AI landscape.
» Confidentiality and privilege are distinct risks. Confidentiality is about data leakage. Privilege is about whether a communication loses its protected status because an AI system was involved, and privilege, once lost, may not be recoverable.
» The privilege position is unsettled. Courts are still working out whether disclosure to an AI tool waives privilege, and the answer seems to turn on whether counsel directed the use, the terms of service of the tool, and whether the jurisdiction treats the AI as a third party. A vetted firm tool under a proper data processing agreement sits in a different risk category from a consumer chatbot.
» An AI use policy that only prohibits tools will push usage underground. Effective policies make compliance easier than non-compliance by setting out what lawyers can do, where they can do it, and which tools are out of bounds.

What to Do with This

» Apply the same three-pillar mitigation to every risk you identify. First, education so lawyers understand how a tool handles data. Second, prevention through technical controls, such as data loss prevention or blocking of specific features. Third, safe alternatives such as on-premises or private-cloud deployments so that lawyers can experiment freely within the firm's firewall.

» Lead client conversations about AI rather than waiting for them. Pair a relationship partner with an innovation professional so that the client hears about both the commercial context and the technical credibility. The most restrictive clients often become advocates once they see that the firm understands the technology.
» Give the policy an owner and a review cycle aligned to AI Committee meetings. A stale AI use policy is worse than no policy because it creates the illusion of governance.
» Involve risk teams early, not after the fact. A firm that can point to a process signed off by its risk function is in a different position from one whose innovation team made the call alone.

Questions to Sit With

» Who is watching for the material changes your vendors release, and how do those changes reach the people who need to know?
» Do your lawyers know the difference between a confidentiality issue and a privilege issue in their AI use, or are the two being treated as a single 'data' concern?
» If you were to put your AI use policy on a single page, could a lawyer read it quickly and leave knowing what they can do, where, and what is off limits?

CHAPTER 9

Lawyer-Built Solutions and Shadow AI

Most of the time, the best innovation within law firms does not emanate from innovation teams. That is a deliberately provocative statement, but it reflects that the most significant innovations in how law is practised do not come from a centralized business function but from the practising lawyers throughout the firm. Innovation teams can help create an environment and culture in which change can occur, but it is only the lawyers, who understand their work deeply, that are going to be able to see where technology can transform it. With AI, more lawyers than ever have the tools to act on that insight without waiting for institutional permission.

Lawyers building their own tools is not necessarily new, but it was never as easy as it is now. Previously, it was a path only available to those with coding and software development skills, and it was usually done outside of a law firm environment. Most legal technology companies come about because a lawyer spotted a problem in the way they worked and was not given the freedom or resources to solve it, so they left to find some software engineers and build the solution themselves. Even those lawyers who built solutions with no-code tools within firms had to do so within the strictures of the law firm's technological architecture, and they were probably restrained by the menu of functions permitted by the software.

That started to change in 2025 with the rise of 'vibe coding'. There is a reason Collins Dictionary made vibe coding its 2025 word of the year (despite it being two words).[1] Put simply, vibe coding is the practice of creating software through conversational prompts rather than through traditional programming. It often goes hand in hand with shadow AI, which is the use of AI tools outside of official organization channels. Like it or not, lawyers within firms and, importantly, in-house teams are using commercially available tools from frontier labs to experiment and build solutions even if the organization they belong to separately subscribes to a proprietary legal AI tool.

How organizations respond to this is important. Amid an explosion of opportunity, prohibition would be unwise. The better response is for organizations to establish a framework that harnesses the passion of individual innovation while managing the risks it creates. Creating a safe space in which people can experiment is crucial.

For lawyers, vibe coding represents something fundamental: it is the collapse of the barrier between the people who understand the work and the people who build the tools.

THE DEMOCRATIZATION OF BUILDING

Until very recently, a lawyer who spotted a workflow worth automating or a process worth improving but who did not want to leave their day job had two options. They could lobby for budget to buy a tool, or they could push for someone to be hired to build one. Either way, the answer was wait.

That wait might now be over, as tools now exist that allow a lawyer with no programming background to describe what they want and create functional software. A lawyer can describe a workflow in plain language and build what they need, removing the need to understand or write code.

The popularity of the proposition is explosive, not just for legal but more widely: Base44, one of the first vibe coding platforms, was acquired by website company Wix for $80 million after just six months of operation by a single developer.[2]

The term vibe coding originates with AI researcher Andrej Karpathy, who used it to describe a new relationship with code; one focused on intent and iteration rather than on understanding every line.[3] In legal application, it means that a partner can now prototype a solution over the course of an evening. An associate can build a tool over a weekend that addresses a specific pain point in their practice. A knowledge lawyer can create a workflow that captures institutional expertise in a form that is immediately usable. None of these people needs to understand programming, they need only understand their own work.

This does, of course, pose risks, particularly in law firms. We have already mentioned that every practice within a law firm functions almost as its own separate business, and that each partner within that practice will have their own way of doing things. The risk of each lawyer having the ability to build their own tools means that the same problem might be solved in ten different ways across a business. This means the firm cannot benefit from the economies of scale of rolling out such solutions, not to mention the issues of infrastructure, governance, and (importantly) security. If the code breaks or a connection to an internal or external source falters, someone has to fix it. Without a central team who are aware of the various solutions and how they work, this will be difficult. It will be even more difficult if the original vibe coder leaves the business and has not engaged in good practices in documenting their process.

Emerging risks aside, true and meaningful innovation happens when practising lawyers – the people who understand the substance of the work – are empowered to build. Innovation and IT teams play a critical role in infrastructure, governance, and scaling, but the creative spark, the identification of what needs to exist, comes from those who actually practise law.

THE COMMERCIAL STAKES: THE CANNIBALIZATION QUESTION

Vibe coding raises an uncomfortable question for some firms, which is what happens when internally built tools (or simply a lawyer set loose on the firm's enterprise licence to Anthropic's Claude Cowork) compete with the firm's own revenue-generating services? When centralized solutions are deployed, leadership can generally align those tools with the strategy and direction of the firm. If individual lawyers are making their own solutions, though, their goals may differ from the strategy. They might be making a process more efficient so that they can focus on more interesting work. This is fine for the lawyer, but what if this is a piece of work for which the firm has previously been able to bill for every hour spent without any questions from the client?

There were a number of instances in the early days of AI where lawyers started completing tasks for clients much faster than they had previously. They then billed that client for the new time spent, excited to build their relationship and to showcase their efficiency. Without the firm having discussed value-based pricing or some other alternative that satisfied both parties, that revenue stream is forever altered.

The most concrete example of how firms might deal with vibe coding is how eDiscovery is delivered. Several large firms maintain significant eDiscovery practices that generate substantial revenue. If a lawyer builds an AI-powered document review tool, or if a general-purpose AI platform begins to offer capabilities that overlap with dedicated eDiscovery tools, the firm faces a tension between innovation and revenue protection.

The pull between wanting to be innovative and not wanting to dilute existing revenue streams is not new. Every industry that has been disrupted by technology has faced the cannibalization question, and the answer from those other industries is consistent: if you do not cannibalize your own revenue, someone else will. The question is not whether AI will transform eDiscovery and other technology-adjacent legal services, it is whether the firm will lead that transformation or be displaced by it.

The practical response to these tensions is awareness and planning. Firms should understand where their revenue is vulnerable to AI-driven disruption, have a strategy for evolving those services, and ensure that internal innovation efforts are coordinated with commercial strategy. New capabilities should be incorporated into strategy and offerings rather than letting them undermine existing revenue without replacement. All legal teams should be thinking about how to encourage vibe coding in a manner where they can maintain awareness. That awareness depends, in the first instance, on knowing what lawyers are building and using. Which brings us to shadow AI.

SHADOW AI: THE INVISIBLE ADOPTION CURVE

Shadow AI is the use of AI tools outside of official firm channels. A lawyer who uses a personal ChatGPT account to draft a memo is engaging in shadow AI; an associate who uploads a contract to Claude to get a first-pass review is doing likewise. Even a partner using an AI research tool they discovered independently, without going through the firm's procurement process, is engaging in shadow AI.

The name makes it sound as if it is something that is hidden, but it is happening at every organization in almost every legal team. The question is not whether it is occurring but whether the organization knows about it, and whether the organization has created conditions that make it unnecessary.

From a risk perspective, shadow AI creates genuine concerns. Files uploaded to personal accounts might be stored in ways that are inconsistent with firm policy. Consumer-grade AI tools might train on user inputs and expose sensitive client data. Lawyers may inadvertently waive attorney–client privilege by processing confidential information through unsanctioned platforms. And, as discussed in the previous chapter, the proliferation of agent-based tools creates the risk that lawyers grant AI systems broad access to their computers and networks without understanding the security implications.

But from an innovation perspective, shadow AI represents something valuable: lawyers solving their own problems. When a lawyer circumvents the official process to use an AI tool, they are demonstrating initiative, identifying a need that the firm's approved tools do not meet, and acting on it. That energy should be captured, not crushed.

GOVERNING THE BUILD: FRAMEWORKS, NOT PROHIBITION

Organizations have several options when confronted with vibe coding and shadow AI. The first, ignoring it, is not really a viable choice at all. The problem with burying your head in the sand is that it will not stop people from doing it. In fact, without any sort of acknowledgement at all, they are likely to use it in a way that triggers all of the risks discussed above.

The second option is to prohibit it. This approach has a superficial appeal as it appears to manage the risk by eliminating the activity. Websites can be blocked on a firm's systems, and strict access provisions can be put in place. But we have already talked about prohibition not being a reasonable mitigation option. Prohibition does not eliminate the activity, it simply drives it underground. If sites are blocked, people will just use their personal devices as these tools are widely available. Talented lawyers who want to build and innovate will either do it secretly, incurring all of the risks that shadow AI creates, or they will leave for firms that give them the space to create.

The final and preferred option is to embrace vibe coding within a framework, therefore eliminating the concept of any use of AI being shadow AI. This means acknowledging that lawyers are building; creating supervised environments where they can do so safely; and establishing processes to evaluate, improve, and scale the most promising innovations.

The framework approach requires a sandbox environment where lawyers can experiment freely without risking client data or firm security. This can be a dedicated instance of a coding tool, a private environment with synthetic data, or a governed workspace within the firm's infrastructure. The key is that it exists, that lawyers know about it, and that it is easy to use.

This approach also requires a known pathway from prototype to product. The most effective approach is often not to maintain the lawyer-built tool indefinitely but to migrate its functionality into supported infrastructure, including proper support for security, data governance, error handling, and scalability. The innovation team's role here is not to gatekeep but to elevate: to take a promising prototype and make it enterprise-grade. If a lawyer builds a contract analysis tool using Claude Code, the firm might take the concept and hand it to its development team or seek to implement it within its preferred third-party platform, whether that is Legora, Harvey, DeepJudge, or another tool with the infrastructure to support ongoing maintenance and updates. The lawyer gets the benefit immediately. The firm gets a supported, scalable version over time.

BUILD, BUY, OR RENT, REVISITED

The rise of vibe coding may, down the line, force a reconsideration of the build-versus-buy (answer: rent) decisions discussed in chapter 7. The traditional framings assume that building is expensive and slow, requiring dedicated development resources. Vibe coding makes building fast and cheap, but it does not make it sustainable.

A tool built by a lawyer using conversational AI is, in effect, a startup with one client (the lawyer). The lawyer who built it will not maintain it indefinitely. They will get bored or they will find themselves busy with billable work, and they will move on. The tool might break when the underlying model changes, when the firm's systems are updated, or when the use case evolves. Without ongoing maintenance, the tool becomes a liability rather than an asset.

In chapter 7 the discussion was about whether to build, buy, or rent in a more traditional sense – the types of solution that might be bought for a practice, a team, or a whole organization. Here, the question arises in relation to smaller, lawyer-built solutions. But the answer is the same: the best solution is often to rent, treating lawyer-built tools as prototypes that prove a concept and then migrating that concept into commercially maintained products or allowing the firm's development team to take it over for maintenance. A technology solution must be maintained by teams of engineers who will update the product, fix bugs and ensure compatibility with evolving firm infrastructure. A lawyer's weekend project, however brilliant, cannot offer that.

This logic holds for now, but it assumes that the destination for a lawyer's idea is always a piece of software, whether that be maintained by firm dev teams or handed to a third-party vendor. However, if the model providers evolve their products to the point where the work can be done directly on a foundation model without anything being built at all, the build, buy, or rent framing may itself become obsolete. We turn to that possibility next.

THE OPEN QUESTION: WILL FIRMS NEED VENDORS?

As vibe coding tools become more powerful and more accessible, will firms continue to invest in external legal AI platforms? There is no clear answer to this question. Large-scale legal platforms such as Harvey and Legora offer integrated capabilities, enterprise security, ongoing maintenance, and a breadth of functionality that no collection of lawyer-built tools can replicate at scale. The annual licence fee, however significant, buys infrastructure that the firm probably could not build and maintain for less. What these platforms do not allow for is tailoring. If the market is dominated by a few software providers, then they will be too big to make changes to account for the way that one organization does business, and integrations will be slow and cumbersome. For law firms in particular, if the competitive advantage in the world of AI is going to rest on proprietary data and custom agents, then subscribing to the same platform as every other firm and your clients is unlikely to provide anything meaningful.

Another perspective is a future in which firms shift the majority of investment from external platforms to internal capability. This would see teams composed of lawyer subject-matter experts paired with engineers equipped with enterprise tools such as Claude Code, i.e. tools that are not legal-specific but do offer robust security and maintenance. These teams could build custom solutions tailored precisely to the firm's needs. In this future, the legal AI platforms become less necessary, and the renewal conversation becomes more difficult.

But building in this way could turn out to be the bridge, not the destination. A lawyer using Anthropic's Claude Cowork for a task does not even actually need to vibe code a replacement product for a third-party tool, and they might not even need the firm's development team behind them either. They describe the task to Cowork and the agent does as instructed, delivering legal work output without the traditional software experience. Vibe coding gave lawyers the ability to create their own solutions for the first time, but agentic tools designed for knowledge work are already making that step unnecessary for many tasks. The gap between what a legal-specific vendor offers and what a lawyer can accomplish with an agent is narrowing not because lawyers have learned to build, but because software (as traditionally understood) might no longer need to be built at all.

The likely outcome is a hybrid. Some firms will keep third-party platform subscriptions for the broad, general-purpose capabilities they provide, while others will build their own. A third possibility is essentially the return of the point solution concept. Point solutions held appeal for lawyers because, as we have discussed, different practices have very different needs, and a general-purpose legal AI platform is never going to be as good at accommodating the quirks of an insurance practice as a tool built for that practice alone. What is killing point solutions is the sprawl. Every tool has its own login, its own interface, its own training curve. A non-legal enterprise technology such as Gemini or Claude sits on top of the stack as an agentic orchestrator: a single environment that can call out to whichever specialized tool or knowledge source is right for the task and bring the result back to the lawyer in one place. The lawyer asks a question or starts a piece of work in one interface. Behind the scenes, the orchestrator routes the contract review piece to the contract review tool, the research piece to the research tool, and the drafting piece to the drafting tool, and it then hands the lawyer back something coherent. The sprawl problem goes away; the specialization stays.

In this model, the longevity concern from the previous section looks different. A lawyer's individual workflow that serves as one component behind an orchestrator does not need to be enterprise-grade, so it does not need to be handed off for longevity. All it needs to do is work well enough, for long enough, to be useful to that lawyer. If it breaks, the lawyer can rebuild it in an afternoon. The disposability that made standalone lawyer-built tools a liability becomes manageable when the orchestrator provides a fallback. Some can live behind the orchestrator as long as they are useful and be replaced when they are not.

Whatever combination emerges, an increasing share of legal work will be shaped by lawyers who understand their practice deeply enough to direct the technology, whether that means building a tool or directing an agent to do the work. The firms that thrive will be those that create the infrastructure to support both paths.

IN-HOUSE TEAMS: A DIFFERENT VERSION OF THE SAME PROBLEM

The principles discussed in this chapter also apply to in-house legal departments, but the pressures are different in ways that matter.

For in-house teams, the cannibalization question is less about revenue and more about headcount and budget. Every efficiency is a boost to the underlying organization and a reduction of costs that might reflect well strategically, but it might also lead the business to conclude that it needs fewer lawyers in the legal department.

The shadow AI risk also takes a different form in-house. The concern here is not just lawyers using unsanctioned tools but people outside of legal building tools that perform legal functions without the legal team's awareness. This might be procurement teams building solutions that review incoming supplier contracts against previously agreed positions. Or it might be teams creating updated employment contracts for hiring by using AI to draft. Although these outputs may for the most part be fit for purpose, those teams might not be aware of legal updates or underlying changes to the way in which contracts are drafted, and as such they might unwittingly get the business into trouble. Centralized legal tools allow the legal team visibility of the whole, while decentralized AI solutions sacrifice that for easier paths to building for other teams. Of course, this is often not a choice the legal team can control, because the AI tool and the architecture that are in place will be a commercial decision of the business. The best thing that legal teams can do in these instances is to become more embedded into the strategic direction of the firm and ensure that the C-suite knows the legal implications of AI.

In-house teams also face constraints that law firms do not. They generally have smaller budgets; they are already advising across a number of practice areas; and instead of buying legal-specific tools, they often have to use whatever existing solutions the business has licensed without the dedicated support a practice would get within a law firm. The build-versus-rent question resolves differently when the in-house team has neither the budget for a legal AI platform nor the internal engineering support to maintain anything complex. For many in-house teams, the most practical path may be exactly the one this chapter describes as the destination: working directly in a general-purpose model, with no legal-specific software layer at all.

RECOGNIZING AND REWARDING INNOVATION

As discussed in chapter 6, if firms want lawyers to innovate, they must recognize and reward the right behaviour. A lawyer who spends an evening building a tool that saves their practice group hundreds of hours has created significant value. Under a traditional billable hour model, that evening was unbillable. Worse, the tool they built might reduce the firm's revenue by making future work faster. The incentive structure actively discourages the behaviour the firm wants to encourage.

The lawyers most inclined to build are often motivated by the satisfaction of solving problems, by the recognition of their peers, and by the opportunity to shape how their practice operates. Firms that celebrate successful innovations, that share them across the organization, and that give credit where it is due will find that innovation begets innovation.

But financial incentives matter too. A lawyer who spends significant time on non-billable innovation and sees it reflected negatively in their annual review will stop innovating. Firms must ensure that their compensation and evaluation structures do not penalize the behaviour they want to encourage. This could mean adjusting billable hour targets for recognized innovators, creating alternative evaluation criteria for lawyers involved in tool building, or establishing innovation as a formal component of the path to partnership.

LOOKING AHEAD

The trajectory of this chapter tells a story in three stages. The first stage, already well underway, is lawyers using AI tools to do their work faster and better. The second, which this chapter has examined at length, is lawyers building their own tools, collapsing the barrier between the people who understand the work and the people who create the technology. The third, still emerging, is lawyers who do not need to build at all, instead directing agentic tools by describing what they want and letting the model handle the rest.

No stage replaces the one before it. There will be lawyers using, lawyers building, and lawyers directing, and this might often be the same person on the same day depending on the task. The firms that respond to this shift with curiosity and structure and those that create the environments, incentives, and governance frameworks to support all three will capture enormous value. Those that treat any one stage as the final answer, or that respond with prohibition rather than adaptation, will lose their most talented and ambitious people to firms that do not.

IN PRACTICE

In a Sentence

The best ideas for how AI should transform legal work come from practising lawyers, and the question is whether your organization captures that creativity or lets it leak out as shadow AI.

What to Remember

» Vibe coding has removed the barrier between the people who understand the work and the people who build the tools. For the first time, a lawyer with an idea can describe it in plain language and have working software within days.

» Shadow AI shows where adoption has outpaced governance. Prohibition drives it underground and pushes the lawyers most interested in AI towards firms that handle it better.
» Look for where tasks could be supplanted by AI or a competitor. If you fail to do this review, someone else will do it for you.
» Treat a lawyer-built tool as a prototype rather than a product. The job of the innovation and IT team is to take the prototypes that matter and rebuild them on proper infrastructure, with the security, support, ownership, and governance that a production system requires.
» Innovation does not survive without recognition. If compensation and promotion criteria do not adjust for the people building tools, the building will stop, or the people doing it will leave.

What to Do with This

» Identify which parts of your revenue are most exposed to AI-driven disruption and decide, explicitly, whether you are going to disrupt them yourself.
» Provide a sandbox in which lawyers can build things safely. No risk of client data leakage, no security risk, and a clear path from working prototype to production-grade tool. The firm's role is to see what is being built, not to control every facet of it.
» Make sure your compensation and promotion system recognizes the lawyers who build. Adjusted billable hour targets, explicit innovation components in review criteria, or a non-traditional partnership track for legal engineers are all options.
» Decide where your agentic orchestration layer will live before you decide which legal AI platform to procure.

General-purpose development tools are increasingly capable of hosting legal workflows. That changes the shape of procurement decisions.

Questions to Sit With

» Which of your most profitable services would an AI-fluent lawyer be able to deliver a first version of? What do you do about that? Do you know how many of your lawyers are building their own tools? Have you asked?

» Is your firm the place your most AI-curious lawyer wants to build, or are you at risk of them leaving?

» Are you tracking the gap between what your legal-specific AI vendors offer and the frontier models? Where does your team think the advantage will be in two years' time?

CHAPTER 10

Working Together

Let us start in the future and work backwards. As mentioned in chapter 1, one possible future is that in a few years' time, law firms will serve their clients via technology, by 'transmitting' the firm's knowledge and skills to address each client's needs, within the client's own environment. In this future, law firms that are not able to meet their clients where they are will be irrelevant for most of their clients' needs.

The legal profession has always been, at least in theory, a collaborative endeavour. Lawyers pride themselves on their relationships with their clients. Teams of lawyers (and firms' business services professionals) are staffed on matters. Different practices work together to achieve a single goal for a client.

Yet for all this apparent collaboration, the underlying model has historically been fragmented. Work has been passed, handed off, reviewed, and returned, often across organizational boundaries that were never designed for such easy exchange. Emails became the blood flowing through the arteries of legal work, and those arteries are clogged with attachments and outdated document versions flying back and forth. Nobody planned for this; it just became the de facto way of working as time-poor individuals were forced to use the tools at hand to interact with their peers.

The introduction of cloud-based platforms and, more recently, AI has not simply added another tool to the lawyer's toolkit, it has begun to reconfigure the very environment in which legal work takes place. Increasingly, the question is not how individuals collaborate but how systems, organizations, and disciplines interoperate in a shared space. Before AI, some law firms created collaborative environments in which clients could access documents and the tools the firm created, but the difference in terms of both costs and requirements meant that the day-to-day software used by each party remained separate. This is increasingly no longer the case. The shift is subtle in appearance but profound in consequence. We are moving from coordination to more full-fledged integration. The future may be one where law firms and their clients must interact more closely than ever before to understand how best to leverage technology. This shift is not simply technological, it is cultural.

At the centre of this transformation we propose a structure that is both simple and deceptively powerful: a triangle composed of the law firm, the in-house team, and the technology provider. Around and through this triangle runs the infrastructure that enables those three parties to interact, often owned and controlled by none of them individually. It is here, within this configuration, that the future of legal services is being shaped.

THE END OF CONTROL

For much of the profession's history, control has been assumed. Law firms controlled their processes, precedents, and knowledge. Clients controlled their instructions, their data, and their ultimate decisions. Technology, where it existed, was largely internal. Systems were purchased, installed, and managed by IT teams. Updates were infrequent, planned, and predictable. As tools have moved to the cloud, the model for buying software has shifted to software-as-a-service (SaaS). Under this arrangement, the software is not held 'on premises', on the physical computers of the organization. Instead, users are given cloud-based licences to access the tools.

While this presents its own technological questions, that is not our focus. The key thing about the shift to SaaS is that in a SaaS model, control over the software is necessarily lost. No single party determines when a tool evolves. Features appear; interfaces change; capabilities expand. The platform improves continuously, often invisibly, and sometimes disruptively. Instead of IT departments dictating the pace of change, as they did in the past, they respond to it. Lawyers do not 'own' their tools in the traditional sense, instead they subscribe to them. This has two immediate consequences.

First, technology providers become active participants in the delivery of legal services, not merely suppliers of background infrastructure. Their design choices shape workflows. Their security models influence data sharing. Their integrations form the capabilities that are available to the users. Their roadmaps determine what is possible.

Second, collaboration becomes unavoidable. When multiple parties rely on the same or interoperable platforms, the boundaries between them become more porous. Work is no longer transferred, it is co-developed; documents are not sent, they are shared, so that analysis is not sequential, but rather, it is concurrent.

It is also worth asking whether the SaaS model itself is as permanent as it appears. The transition to cloud-based subscriptions is well established, but the businesses built on top of that model face increasing pressure. As the cost of building software drops, platforms that relied on the complexity of their code as a competitive advantage may find that advantage disappearing. A capable legal engineer with access to a foundation model can now build in weeks what once took a funded startup years to develop, and lawyers themselves can do substantive work directly, or build skills in tools such as Claude without needing a legal-specific vendor product at all. The pressure intensifies as foundation model companies move beyond selling infrastructure. Anthropic's Claude is now embedded in the Microsoft 365 environment, from Excel to Word,[1] and both Anthropic and OpenAI are building product layers directly on top of their own models that appeal directly to the legal community. (Anthropic doing so overtly, in May 2026, with the launch of Claude for Legal.) In Spring 2026 Microsoft launched a 'Legal Agent' directly in Word, adding itself to the list of 'tech giants' targeting the legal vertical. When a frontier model provider or legacy enterprise platform becomes the legal tech product, a third-party vendor has to justify why it is still in the room. The investment climate that funded rapid expansion in legal technology is also shifting. Vendors whose value lies in deep domain expertise, proprietary data, and trusted relationships will adapt. Those whose value was primarily in the software itself may not. Firms building long-term strategy around specific platforms should account for the possibility that some of those platforms will not be around in their current form, if at all, five years from now.

None of this means vendors disappear tomorrow. For now, and probably for the medium term, they remain central to how legal work is delivered. But the ground beneath them is shifting, and that instability shapes every relationship in the model that follows.

THE TRIANGLE OF TRANSFORMATION

The law firm, the client, and the vendor have always existed in relation to one another. What has changed is the intensity and immediacy of that relationship. Each of the triangle's three corners brings something distinct that the others do not.

The law firm contributes legal expertise, experience, and judgement. It interprets the law, navigates complexity, and advises on risk. The client provides context, commercial understanding, and strategic direction. It defines the problem, sets priorities, and ultimately determines value. The vendor brings capability. It builds the tools, maintains the infrastructure, and increasingly shapes how legal work is performed. Individually, each is necessary. Together, they become transformative.

Historically, these relationships were mediated. The client instructed the firm; the firm selected and deployed technology; the vendor remained at a distance. Today, those lines are blurred. Clients are increasingly selecting or mandating specific platforms or capabilities from their firms. Vendors might engage directly with clients and firms simultaneously. Law firms may co-develop solutions with both. Vendors are hiring legal talent directly from law firms and in-house teams to create use cases and functionality, and to forge their own relationships.

The result is a shift from bilateral relationships to a genuinely triangular dynamic. Decisions made at one corner reverberate across the others. A change in a platform affects both firm and client workflows. A client's technology strategy influences which firms it engages. A firm's approach to innovation affects how vendors design and deploy their tools. This is an important element of change: it is not just occurring in the actual tasks that are being done but in the interactions between the people in the profession. To ignore this shift and focus solely on the new technological capabilities of AI is a mistake. Although technological advancement has driven change, relationships will shape what the end point of this change looks like.

The triangle is a useful model but it should not be mistaken for a symmetrical one. The three corners do not exert equal force. Even the largest and most well-capitalized legal AI vendors remain modest in scale when measured against the institutional weight of a major law firm. A firm's business development infrastructure alone may employ as many people as the most sophisticated vendor organization, and those professionals bring decades of embedded client relationships, sector expertise, and commercial judgement that cannot be replicated quickly. When those same professionals are then also properly augmented by AI, the result may be a strengthened institution, not a weakened one. The vendor corner of the triangle is important, but the sheer depth of capital, talent, and institutional knowledge inside large firms deserves more weight in the model than an evenly drawn triangle might suggest.

COMMUNICATION AS INFRASTRUCTURE

In this environment, communication ceases to be a soft skill and becomes an operational necessity. It is no longer sufficient for lawyers to explain their reasoning clearly to a client, they must also ensure that data flows without friction between organizations, that processes on both sides are aligned, and that the systems used by each party can work together effectively.

Reporting is a central part of this shift. Legal departments are now fully integrated parts of the business and must justify their costs accordingly. The relationship between a firm and a client can no longer rest solely on the personal connection between a general counsel and a partner. The business will want the best value for money, the best track record in terms of outcomes, and demonstrable investment in the client relationship. Matter cycle times, cost predictability, and adoption of agreed workflows are all becoming part of the selection and retention conversation.

Translation is equally important because lawyers must be able to articulate legal requirements in terms that technologists can implement, so that solutions integrate with the client's systems and ways of working and also produce the right reporting and analytics. Vendors must understand the practical realities of legal work. Clients must bridge both, ensuring that what gets built aligns with business objectives. In-house teams increasingly want their technology specialists speaking directly to the firm's technology specialists, which signals that the technical dimension of a relationship is becoming as important as the purely legal one. The most effective teams treat communication not as an adjunct to delivery but as its foundation.

RETHINKING VALUE

As collaboration broadens and deepens, the way in which legal services are evaluated begins to change. For decades, law firms have relied on a combination of expertise, reputation, and relationships to secure work. These factors remain relevant, but they are no longer sufficient on their own. Clients have access to more information than ever before. They can assess performance through data, compare providers with greater ease, and benchmark outcomes across matters.

What clients increasingly want to see is both legal excellence and evidence of how that excellence is delivered. They want to know whether the firm has worked on similar matters, whether it understands their industry, and whether it can navigate the specific challenges at hand. But they also want to know how AI is being deployed, what additional services are available to them, and whether the firm can integrate into their working environment. Selection is becoming multidimensional in a way that it was not before.

This has consequences for how firms present themselves. The reputation of a firm will no longer be built solely on past success and legal technical ability. Those will form part of a wider picture that includes technology capability, adaptability, and the willingness to collaborate in new ways. Firms that can demonstrate these qualities through concrete metrics rather than general assurances will have an advantage. Client satisfaction scores, matter cycle times, and cost predictability are becoming part of the conversation, not as replacements for judgement and expertise, but as evidence that judgement and expertise are being applied effectively. There will also be a push towards more multidisciplinary teams on matters, stretching beyond just lawyers being staffed, as firms look to show clients the full range of what they can bring.

THE CHANGING SHAPE OF COMPETITION

One of the most significant consequences of AI is the democratization of capability. Historically, scale has been a defining advantage for law firms. Larger firms could invest in resources, build extensive knowledge bases, and deploy teams across jurisdictions.

Smaller firms, while often more agile, struggled to compete on breadth. Take a simple legal technology example of a firm preparing a bespoke global survey for a client that contains the latest employment laws in key jurisdictions. Launching the first version requires liaising with multiple local counsel to establish that the law is correct, along with a considerable degree of coordination. On top of that, maintaining such a service has always been a time sink that could take a whole team of paralegals. But now that service can be created and maintained by the use of agents that require much less supervision. In this way, technology begins to erode the scale advantage.

Access to sophisticated tools is also no longer limited to the largest organizations. Cloud-based platforms, AI-driven analysis, and modular systems allow smaller teams to operate with a level of capability that was previously unattainable. Knowledge can be structured, accessed, and applied more efficiently. Processes can be standardized and automated using Microsoft tools such as the Power Platform and Copilot Studio without having to buy costly legal-specific point solutions. While this does not eliminate the advantages of scale entirely, it does alter the landscape.

Smaller firms and teams can now compete more effectively, particularly in areas where agility and specialization are valued. Individual lawyers, supported by the right infrastructure, might become more prominent in attracting work. The brand of the firm remains important but it is no longer the sole determinant. The levelling effect of AI also has a ceiling. The same tools available to a five-person practice are being deployed inside firms with dedicated AI teams, proprietary data architectures, and the budget to build deeply integrated workflows. Scale does not just mean more people. It means the ability to invest in infrastructure that compounds over time.

There is also a secondary effect worth naming, which is that as AI delivers on its efficiency promises, in-house teams will face pressure on headcount, and as a result their organizations will likely consolidate their panels. When that happens, the firms best positioned to survive the cut will be those that can demonstrate AI capability at an institutional level, not simply at the level of individual tools. That favours the firms with the resources to have committed early and at scale. Although, as we said earlier, legal technical ability is likely to become only part of law firm selection, if all other things are equal in terms of technological capability, then the quality of the people will be more important than the quantity of them.

This raises an intriguing possibility: a future in which clients prioritize individuals and teams over institutions. Such a shift would not be absolute. Institutions provide stability, governance, and a breadth of capability that remains valuable. But the balance may change. Clients may seek out those who can integrate seamlessly into their environment, regardless of the size of the organization they represent. This would cause a larger shock in England and Wales (where lawyers have been more willing to see a firm as a business rather than a collection of individuals) than it would in the United States, but it would change how things are done everywhere.

There is an argument that this could end up like the structure used for barristers in England and Wales, where a series of independent self-employed legal professionals band together under the auspices of a 'chambers' so that work can be coordinated and shared between them. As the chambers are not businesses, there are tensions with investments into overheads and technology, but if AI truly becomes democratized, then this may not pose the issue it once did.

With the caveat that running a legal matter is not the same as driving a taxi, Uber made it possible for independent drivers – who had previously been associated with taxi firms to get work – to be listed directly on the company's app, with no affiliation. One future could be a similar service that allows star lawyers to get work based on their own reputation without being part of a well-reputed firms.

KNOWLEDGE, DATA, AND THE EROSION OF MOATS

If capability becomes more widely accessible, what then constitutes a competitive advantage? Traditionally, proprietary knowledge and data have been seen as defensible moats. Legal databases, internal precedents, and accumulated experience provided differentiation. Yet as technology evolves, these moats may become less secure.

Data can increasingly be connected across systems. Many external knowledge sources provide access to their knowledge via APIs. These are structured access routes into the tools. The advent of MCP, though, means that AI can 'think' its way around those knowledge bases in a much more adaptive and capable way. AI tools can integrate multiple sources, combining proprietary and public information, and models can analyse and synthesize data at scale, reducing the advantage of any single repository.

This does not render data irrelevant, though. On the contrary, it actually increases its importance, but the value shifts from ownership to utilization. The ability to curate, interpret, and apply data becomes more significant than simply possessing it. Interoperability becomes key. Systems that can connect, exchange, and build upon data from multiple sources offer greater flexibility. Those that remain siloed may struggle to keep pace.

In this context, the role of knowledge management, legal technology, and governance becomes central to the 'rainmaker' proposition. It is no longer sufficient to bring in work; one must also demonstrate the ability to track it, store it, recall it, and deliver it effectively within a complex ecosystem.

WHERE WORK HAPPENS: THE CLIENT-CENTRIC ENVIRONMENT

If collaboration is the defining feature of the new model, then the question of where work happens becomes critical. By this, we do not mean the *physical* location. We have no interest in getting into a debate about whether people work from home or in the office. What we mean is the *digital* location. The traditional answer has been fragmented. Law firms work within their own systems; clients operate within theirs. When information is exchanged, it is through portals, emails, and document management systems. A series of versions is thrown 'over the fence' until the other party needs to see it. That model is increasingly inefficient.

Extranets and static portals, once heralded as the future, possess limitations. These single platforms struggle to keep pace with the demands of modern collaboration. They are often clunky, disconnected, and underutilized, and they also require in-house teams to visit numerous different environments for each of their firms, remembering passwords and having no way of taking the information out of those systems to put into their own.

The future points towards platforms where firms and clients can work together directly; where data is accessible within defined permissions; and where tools are embedded into workflows rather than layered on top, akin to the legal streaming-style service discussed earlier in this chapter. Integrated platforms, often within broader ecosystems such as Microsoft or Google, provide a foundation for this kind of collaboration. Tools such as Teams and Copilot hint at what is possible when communication, documentation, and AI capabilities are combined. These environments are not yet perfect. Questions around security, permissioning, and governance remain complex. But the direction of travel is clear.

One of the more radical implications of this shift is the possibility that outside counsel will operate directly within the client's environment. Instead of transferring documents back and forth, lawyers might access client systems, work on shared datasets, and contribute to ongoing workflows. The distinction between internal and external begins to blur.

This model offers clear advantages. It reduces friction for the in-house team. Information does not need to be duplicated or transferred and context can be retained across numerous matters and firms. Collaboration becomes more immediate as the client has ready access instead of having to navigate to an external site. It also enhances transparency: clients can see progress in real time, understand how work is being performed, and engage more directly with the process. It aligns incentives. When all parties operate within the same environment, there is a greater sense of shared ownership.

However, it also raises challenges. Security and permissioning become paramount. Not all data can or should be shared. Systems must be designed to allow granular control over access. The problem of access that was previously encountered by in-house teams has now shifted to law firms, who have to navigate between client systems. Governance becomes more complex. Who is responsible for maintaining the environment? How are changes managed? What happens when relationships end?

Prompts, outputs, and custom agent ownership are emerging examples of this complexity. Some clients now regard these as their intellectual property. If a firm develops a tailored series of prompts to handle a client's regulatory filings or transaction structure, the client might view those as inseparable from the engagement. They were shaped by the client's data, refined through the client's feedback, and built around the client's specific needs. This is a governance issue that needs to be addressed early in the relationship, ideally before the work begins.

There are also questions about how much transparency is preferred, particularly for firms. There is a reason that firms and clients rarely work in live collaboration platforms such as Google Docs or Microsoft Word 365. Junior lawyers or AI systems might make suggestions that are incorrect and need to be checked before a document moves to a new major version. With the best will in the world, the lawyers on a matter may not release their time until the end of the week, leading to sudden jumps in fees if they are being monitored in real time. This is something that makes client partners uncomfortable. If live collaboration is to be the future, there either needs to be some form of sign-off process built in or law firms and their clients need clear and frank discussions about what is being shared and when things are ready to be reviewed.

Cultural adjustments are also required in an environment where clients, or indeed vendors, directly own the collaboration platforms. Law firms must be willing to operate within systems they do not control. Clients must be comfortable granting access to external parties or sharing granular permissions in a way that firms can use as required. Despite these challenges, the trajectory is compelling and the benefits of integration are difficult to ignore.

There is, however, a commercial counterargument that is worth taking seriously. What a leading firm sells is not simply the accuracy of its advice, it is the full experience of being represented by that institution, including the calibre of the people, the depth of the organization behind them, and the confidence that comes from knowing the matter is in hands that have handled hundreds like it before. Firms that can credibly deliver AI as part of that experience have a strong incentive to draw clients into their own environment, not to disperse their capabilities into a platform they do not control.

Giving clients direct access to the tools and workflows that underpin the advice risks turning a high-value relationship into a commodity transaction. History also offers a cautionary note here. Technology-enabled delivery models have been tested in legal services for more than two decades, and in specific market segments they have found real traction. But the consistent lesson has been that while the technology and the commercial logic tend to be sound, the adoption by the humans inside the model is where things stall. Legal work carries enormous amounts of judgement, nuance, and relationship, and when complexity increases, people tend to revert to what they know. The direction of travel described here is real, but the pace of the shift might be slower than the structural logic alone would predict.

CASE STUDY: THE TRIANGLE IN ACTION

Consider a multinational company undertaking a large-scale acquisition across multiple jurisdictions. The transaction involves complex regulatory approvals, extensive due diligence, and significant commercial risk. The company has instructed Roscoe, Jasper, & Mills LLP as counsel. In a traditional model, RJM would coordinate the work. Documents would be shared through secure portals or email; reviews were conducted using tools internal to the firm; and updates would be provided through reports and calls. The data room would be selected by the selling company in one platform while RJM might have wanted to review with their own tools, extracting the documents out for the purpose. These documents and their outputs might travel between numerous systems for review, analysis, and to produce the required due diligence reports and issue lists.

In a triangular model, the approach is different. The client selects a shared platform as the central environment for the transaction, establishing the requisite permissions. The data sources and workflows that will be used might be provided by the company, by RJM, or by the vendor. This platform integrates document management, AI-driven review tools, and collaboration features. Access is granted to the law firm and maintained by a technology vendor responsible for monitoring and customizing the platform.

Due diligence is conducted within the platform. Documents are either uploaded once and analysed using AI tools provided by the vendor, or they remain in the vendor's systems and are accessed via the AI agents of the client. The law firm reviews and validates the outputs, focusing on areas of complexity and risk. The client's in-house team monitors progress in real time, accessing dashboards that provide insights into key issues. Workflows are triggered on the occurrence of milestone events.

Communication takes place within the platform. Questions are raised and answered in context. Decisions are documented alongside the relevant materials, with a clear audit trail. As the transaction progresses, the client or vendor might update the platform to accommodate new features or workflows. These changes affect both the firm and the client, requiring coordination and communication.

Throughout, the triangle remains active. The law firm provides expertise and judgement. The client provides direction and context. The vendor provides capability and adaptability. The result is a more integrated, efficient, and transparent process. Rather than being passed between parties, work is developed collaboratively. While boundaries between organizations remain, they are less obstructive.

THE ROLE OF TECHNOLOGY PROVIDERS

As the triangle becomes more embedded, the role of providers evolves. They are no longer passive providers of tools. They become partners in delivery. Their decisions influence how legal work is performed, how data is structured, and how collaboration occurs.

This places new demands on vendors, who must understand the legal context in which their tools are used. Generic solutions are often insufficient, so customization, flexibility, and responsiveness become key. The response of vendors has been to hire legal engineers and specialists directly from in-house and law firm teams and to co-create solutions with their users. Complex relationships must then be navigated. Engaging with law firms and clients simultaneously requires sensitivity and clarity. Missteps can create friction and undermine trust.

Vendors must also respect governance structures. Where clients or firms have established innovation functions, these should be engaged rather than bypassed. Attempting to circumvent such structures may accelerate initial adoption but can damage long-term relationships. Contacting partners directly might seem like the best way of implementing a tool, but the partners are not privy to the procurement and security requirements of a tool. For vendors, success lies in understanding the ecosystem, not just the product.

The question behind all this is whether these AI providers will eventually step into the role of legal advisors themselves. The more they understand the ecosystem and the more they operate on common matters, the more likely it becomes that they could move to spin off into a law firm.

As noted in chapter 1, these providers might just be the biggest Trojan Horse in the industry. Several of the most prominent legal AI companies have publicly stated that they do not intend to become law firms, positioning themselves instead as infrastructure that helps firms convert their expertise into scalable AI products. That position is credible and defensible. But the direction in which these businesses are travelling – the growing accumulation of legal knowledge, the recruitment of experienced lawyers from large firms and in-house teams, and the increasingly embedded role in client workflows – generates its own momentum.

Strategic intent and structural trajectory do not always remain aligned. If a vendor were to signal a move into legal services,[2] what had been a productive partnership could become a direct competitive threat overnight. Firms are aware of this. The caution with which many already share data and grant access to these platforms is not irrational. It is a reasonable commercial response to an uncertain future. This chapter has framed vendors as partners in delivery and for now that framing is accurate, but whether it holds is among the more consequential questions the profession will face in the coming years.

HUMAN SKILLS IN A SYSTEMIC WORLD

Amid all this change it is tempting to focus solely on technology, but the human element becomes, if anything, more important, not less. Soft skills are poorly named, as they are often the elements with which people struggle the most. It is becoming increasingly common to call them human skills, which feels like an apt description when technology is so prevalent.

Communication, empathy, adaptability, and collaboration are vitally important in navigating complex, multiparty environments and in conducting change management internally and externally. Understanding the commercial context of your clients and the drivers behind the advice being sought is vital. What makes a lawyer stand out in this context is not just their legal knowledge, but their ability to collaborate and integrate not just technology but people and knowledge into a broader system. To work with technologists. To understand client needs. To adapt to evolving platforms. The most effective professionals are those who can bridge gaps: between law and technology; between firm and client; and between strategy and execution.

There is a further dimension to this. As AI takes on more of the procedural and transactional elements of legal work, the moments where a human is genuinely needed will become more visible, not less. The points in a matter where someone must exercise judgement, absorb ambiguity, and take personal responsibility for a recommendation will stand out more sharply against a backdrop of automated process. There is also a reputational layer to this that should not be underestimated. Large organizations face real consequences when decisions go wrong, and the ability to point to a recognized institution standing behind the advice is itself a form of protection. That dynamic – the institutional credibility that a trusted firm provides to the people who retain it – is something a technology platform is unlikely to replicate in the near term. The transformation described in this book may well make those high-stakes human interactions more consequential rather than less so.

A NEW OPERATING MODEL

Working together, then, is not an optional enhancement to legal practice. It is its emerging operating model. The triangle of law firm, client, and vendor provides the structure. Shared platforms provide the environment. Communication provides the connective tissue.

Within this model, roles evolve. Law firms are not just advisors anymore; increasingly they are collaborators, sometimes orchestrators. Clients become more than recipients of services. They become active participants in design and delivery, and they are likely to be orchestrators themselves. Vendors become more than suppliers. They become partners in capability, having to adapt to the matter and support all sides. While the boundaries between these roles remain, they are ever more permeable.

LOOKING AHEAD

The trajectory of change is clear, even if the destination is not. The pace of technological development will keep accelerating. Platforms will become more sophisticated, and MCP will unlock new forms of integration. Clients will demand greater efficiency, transparency, and value. Some will expect their legal providers to operate within their environments. Others will continue to value the experience of being inside a firm's world, particularly for high-stakes work where institutional credibility and accountability matter as much as the advice itself.

Law firms will need to adapt, investing not only in technology but in the skills and structures required to operate within this evolving model, along with the talent to work in a hybrid world of law and technology. Vendors will continue to innovate, shaping the possibilities of what can be achieved and hiring their own legal experts. Whether those vendors remain partners or become competitors is a question the profession will need to keep watching closely.

The future is still evolving but what can be said with confidence is that the fundamental principle remains unchanged: legal services exist to solve client problems. What is changing is how those problems are solved. Not by individuals working in isolation, nor by organizations operating in silos, but through deeper forms of collaboration that bring together expertise, context, and capability. The firms that lead this transformation will be those that commit to it early and aggressively, with the institutional weight and human judgement to make it work. Working together, in this sense, is not merely a theme, it is the future of the profession.

IN PRACTICE

In a Sentence

The old bilateral relationship between firm and client is giving way to a triangle of firm, client, and technology provider, and the work that used to sit in portals and handoffs is moving into shared environments where all three operate at once.

What to Remember

» SaaS stripped control from any single organization. The firm no longer decides when a tool evolves and neither does the client, and the vendor has become an active participant in delivery rather than being merely a background supplier.
» The triangle is not symmetrical. Firms still hold institutional weight, capital, and most of the client relationships, but the distribution of influence has shifted far enough that a strategy built on bilateral relationships is already outdated.
» Proprietary data on its own is a weaker moat than it used to be. As AI connects across multiple knowledge sources, competitive advantage moves from owning data to curating, interpreting, and applying it within a connected system.
» Work is moving into shared client-centric environments rather than portals and handoffs. This means fewer emails, fewer document exchanges, and more concurrent work in a single workspace. That reduces friction and multiplies governance questions.

» Human skills become more important in a systemic world. The moments that require judgement, ambiguity absorption, and institutional accountability stand out against everything AI does around them. Those moments are what clients pay for.

What to Do with This

» Build translation capacity in your team. Hire and develop people who can move between legal requirements, technical architecture, and commercial context, because that capability is now operational, not a nice-to-have.
» Audit what your organization owns versus what it curates. Build interoperability into your systems so that you can source from multiple places rather than depend on a single proprietary database.
» Run a small shared-environment pilot with one sophisticated client. Establish governance up front on access rights, prompt and output ownership, transparency, and how the relationship ends if it ends. Document what you learn before expanding.
» Treat vendors as collaborators. Build direct technical relationships between your innovation team and your vendors' product teams, and bring your in-house clients' technologists into those conversations.

Questions to Sit With

» How much of your competitive advantage comes from what you own versus how quickly you can assemble, interpret, and apply what others can also access?
» If a major vendor announced tomorrow that it was acquiring a law firm, what would change in how you think about your existing vendor relationships?
» What part of your service delivery would look different if a client asked you to do it entirely inside their environment rather than in yours?

CHAPTER 11

Keeping Up

If you have read this far, you now have a framework for thinking about AI in the practice of law. You understand the strategic considerations, the people implications, the tool landscape, the risk environment, and the governance structures that responsible adoption requires. The question that remains is a practical one. How do you keep up?

This is not a trivial question. Technology is changing daily. The tools available this month may be obsolete by next quarter. People who have spent years building expertise in this area regularly reevaluate their positions, opinions, and strategy as the landscape shifts beneath them. Opinions that were conventional wisdom six months ago are now considered naive, while positions that seemed radical have become mainstream. For someone trying to stay current, the sheer volume of information is overwhelming, and the signal-to-noise ratio is poor.

This chapter provides a snapshot of valuable resources at the time of writing. Specific tools, specific publications, and specific voices will come and go. The goal is to give you a structure for staying current that will outlast any particular product or publication.

PEOPLE AND NETWORKS

For many of the people working in legal innovation and technology, the single most valuable source of information is other people. LinkedIn, whether you love it or hate it, has become the de facto platform where legal technology professionals share what they are learning, what they are building, and what they think is coming next. Following the right people is, for many practitioners, more useful than subscribing to any formal publication. The information is more current, the perspectives are more candid, and the feedback loop is faster. When a new tool launches, or a court issues a decision that affects AI use, or a firm announces a new policy, the analysis appears on LinkedIn before it appears anywhere else. Colin Levy has published a useful list of resources and people to follow in this space, and it is a good starting point for anyone looking to build their network.[1] Perhaps you could start by following the authors of this book:

- linkedin.com/in/adamcurphey,
- linkedin.com/in/ozbenamram, and
- linkedin.com/in/rebeccapasternak.

Within firms, knowledge management and innovation teams play a similar role. They track developments, evaluate tools, and filter the noise so that individual lawyers do not have to do it themselves. If your firm has an innovation function, connecting with it is one of the simplest and most effective things you can do. If your firm does not, or if you are in an in-house team, the question becomes one of what internal resources you can tap into. What are the teams evaluating? What tools are already in the technology stack that you might not know about? Lawyers sometimes assume that because they work in a legal context, they need legal-specific AI tools, but that is not always the case. The tools that the broader organization has already procured, particularly those within the Microsoft ecosystem, might already offer capabilities that lawyers have not explored for very valuable use cases such as collaboration.

For those inclined to build their own systems in order to keep current, the tools now exist to do so without programming expertise. It is possible to set up automated newsletter summaries, RSS feeds, and even trend-tracking dashboards using AI tools and no-code connectors. The output is a personalized briefing, delivered on a schedule, that synthesizes what is happening across multiple sources. This is not necessary, and most people will not do it, but for those who want a structured approach to staying current, the barrier to entry has dropped to near zero. The relevant skills and implications are discussed in chapter 9.

COMMUNITIES

Beyond individual networks, formal communities provide a more structured way to stay current and exchange ideas. The legal technology space has several, and they serve different audiences.

SKILLS.law is a community oriented primarily towards law firms. It brings together innovation professionals, knowledge management leaders, and others responsible for practice technology strategy, and transformation within firms, and provides a forum for sharing experience, benchmarking, and peer learning. For anyone in a law firm who is responsible for or interested in AI strategy, SKILLS is one of the first places to look.

The Corporate Legal Operations Consortium (CLOC)[2] and LegalOps[3] serve a parallel function for in-house legal teams. Both communities focus on the operational side of legal practice, including technology adoption, process improvement, and vendor management. For in-house counsel trying to understand what their peers are doing with AI, or for law firm professionals who want to understand what their clients are thinking, these communities provide direct access to the conversation.

The International Legal Technology Association (ILTA)[4] occupies a broader position in the ecosystem. It serves law firms, in-house teams, and vendors, and its conferences and working groups cover a wide range of legal technology topics. For someone who wants a single community that spans the full landscape, the ILTA is a must-join community.

There are also informal communities, including established regional Knowledge & Innovation meetup groups and newer groups such as LegalQuants,[5] that operate outside the established conference circuit. These tend to be smaller, more experimental, and more focused on emerging applications. They are worth seeking out, particularly for people who are further along in their understanding and want to engage with practitioners who are pushing the boundaries of what is possible.

THE ROLE OF CONSULTANTS

Consultants play a particular role in the legal technology ecosystem that is worth understanding. They function as connectors. And because they work across multiple firms and in-house teams, they see patterns that any single organization cannot. They know what is working at one firm and failing at another. They know which vendors are fulfilling their promises and which are not. They carry information between organizations in a way that internal teams, bound by confidentiality and institutional silos, cannot.

The Legaltech Hub[6] is one example of this kind of role, operating as what one contributor described as 'the garden of legal tech', cultivating connections and tending to the ecosystem instead of selling into it. In-house teams are increasingly turning to consultants not just for implementation support but for market intelligence. When a General Counsel asks a consultant what other companies are doing with AI, the answer is grounded in first-hand observation rather than published surveys, and that makes it more useful.

This is not an endorsement of any particular consultancy. It is an observation that the consulting layer in legal technology serves an information-flow function that is distinct from what communities, publications, or vendors provide. For people trying to keep up, consultants are part of the landscape, and knowing how to use them, whether for formal engagements or informal conversations, is a practical skill.

PROFESSIONAL BODIES AND ASSOCIATIONS

Bar associations, law societies, and their equivalents around the world are increasingly active in the AI space. Many have established AI task forces or legal technology committees that produce guidance, host events, and provide continuing education on the topic.[7] For lawyers who are members of these bodies, participating in or at least following the work of these committees is a straightforward way to stay current on the regulatory and ethical dimensions of AI use in practice.

In the United States, local and state bar associations vary in how much they focus on legal technology, but the recent trend is towards giving it more attention, not less. In England and Wales, the Law Society has conducted surveys on the use of legal technology and publishes regular updates on the topic.[8] There is also the government-backed LawtechUK,[9] which is seeking to drive digital transformation in the legal sector. For sole practitioners and smaller firms in particular, professional bodies can serve a function that larger firms handle internally. They aggregate information, provide guidance, and in some cases offer access to tools and training that a small practice could not develop on its own.

There are also organizations that provide technology infrastructure and oversight specifically for smaller and mid-sized firms. In the United States, firms such as Kraft Kennedy and Harbor Global offer managed IT and technology consulting services that effectively keep their clients current. The firm outsources its technology management to an organization whose job is to stay at the frontier, and the firm benefits without having to build that expertise internally. For sole practitioners and small firms this model can be particularly effective since it addresses the capacity problem that makes keeping up so difficult in the first place.

YOUR OWN TESTING

No amount of reading, networking, or conference attendance substitutes for using the tools yourself. A recurring theme in the conversations that informed this book is that too many lawyers have never actually sat down with an AI tool and tested it on their own work. They have heard about it, they have opinions about it, but they have not used it. The gap between reading about AI and using AI is where most of the fear and misunderstanding lives. Once a lawyer has spent an hour testing a tool on a real question, even in a controlled environment, the abstraction dissolves and the conversation becomes practical.

Chapter 8 discussed the risk framework for this kind of experimentation, and the message bears repeating here. Firms that provide safe environments for testing – where lawyers can use AI without fear of data leakage or professional sanction – will produce lawyers who are better informed, more confident, and more capable of evaluating what they read and hear. Firms that do not provide those environments will produce lawyers whose opinions about AI are formed chiefly by second-hand information and slow procurement cycles. The difference between those two groups will only widen over time.

DEMOS, PILOTS, AND HORIZON SCANNING

Closely related to personal testing is the practice of seeing what others are building. Vendor demonstrations, pilot programmes, and proof-of-concept exercises all provide exposure to capabilities that might not yet be part of the firm's approved toolkit. For innovation teams and procurement professionals, this is already part of the job. For practising lawyers, it is less common but increasingly valuable.

The point of attending a demo is not necessarily to buy anything. It is to update your understanding of what is possible. The pace of product development in legal AI means that assumptions formed even six months ago may be outdated. A tool that could not do something reliably in January may do it well by July. Seeing regular demonstrations, whether they are organized internally or attended at conferences, is one of the simplest ways to recalibrate your sense of what the technology can and cannot do.

PODCASTS AND PUBLICATIONS

There is no shortage of podcasts and publications covering legal technology and AI. Rather than name specific ones, as doing so would inevitably date, the more useful advice is to suggest that you find two or three that match your level of engagement and commit to following them regularly. For someone who is new to the space, a general legal technology podcast that covers developments in an accessible language is a reasonable starting point. For someone who is already active in the field, more technical or niche publications might be more useful.

The key is consistency rather than volume. It is better to follow a small number of sources reliably than to subscribe to everything and read nothing. Most of the well-informed people in this space follow a handful of individuals and publications closely rather than trying to monitor the entire landscape. Find your sources, check them regularly, and supplement with the communities and networks described above when you need to go deeper on a particular topic.

WHAT COMES NEXT

This is a short chapter by design. It is not a comprehensive directory of resources, it is a set of habits and categories. Follow the right people. Join the right communities. Use the tools yourself. See what others are building. Engage with professional bodies. Find a few reliable sources of information and check them regularly. Specific names and platforms will change. Good learning habits will not.

The technology that this book describes is still in its early stages, and the legal profession's engagement with it is even younger. The practitioners who will be best positioned in five years' time are not necessarily the ones who know the most today, they are the ones who have built habits that keep them learning. The most dangerous position is not ignorance, it is the belief that you have learned enough and can stop paying attention. In a field that is changing this fast, staying still is falling behind.

Epilogue: Where Do We Go from Here?

You have now journeyed through eleven chapters of transformation. We started by examining why and how the legal profession is shifting beneath our feet: the economics of the billable hour may truly no longer work; the expectations of clients are evolving; and the technology is genuinely capable of handling tasks that once required specialized expertise. And we then moved through the fundamentals, such as how AI actually works, why understanding it matters, and why the technology is not the scary black box that many fear.

From there, we explored the organizational dimension by examining strategy and pricing, team structure, data as the true work product, training and adoption, tool selection, risk and governance, the democratization of building, the importance of collaboration, and the habit of continuous learning. We have touched on everything from the trivial to the profound. If there is one arc to this book, it is that success is not about the tool but rather about alignment between seemingly unrelated things that must come together to compose the future.

You are not reading this book in a stable moment. The legal profession is in flux. AI has accelerated a shift that was already underway, with clients expecting more value for less money, partners expecting new revenue or cost reduction, and employees having questions and expecting to be heard about what changes mean for their work. And yes, there is genuine uncertainty about what skills will matter in two years, five years, or ten.

This closing note is both a reflection and a call to action. We know the landscape is uncertain. We know the pace of change will not slow. But we also believe that firms and teams that approach this thoughtfully and that treat AI adoption as a holistic organizational transformation, not merely technology implementation, will thrive because they asked the right questions.

INTEGRATION, NOT INSTALLATION

We have consistently reemphasized what we believe to be core tenets to success throughout this book, including that buying a tool is not a strategy, installing software is not a transformation, and a proof of concept is not a plan.

We have all seen it. A firm buys the latest AI tool, rolls it out to everyone, and then wonders why adoption rates are low, quality is inconsistent, and the ROI does not materialize. This may lead to the blame game. The leadership team points to the tool vendor. The employees say they were not trained properly. Nothing changes – or worse, confidence erodes.

The firms and teams that are succeeding with AI are those that have answered a deeper set of questions first.

- What do we want to do differently?
- What problems are we actually trying to solve?
- What does success look like for our clients, our team, our business?
- How do we price and bill work in this new paradigm?
- Do we have the data we need?
- Is that data trustworthy and well-organized such that we can unplug it from one tool and plug it into another as needed?
- Do our people understand why this matters, or are we just telling them to use the tool?
- Are we building governance that enables or governance that suffocates?
- What are the real risks, as opposed to the imagined ones?

The technology you choose to invest in is the enabler, but the overarching strategy, the data, the culture, and the architectural governance are the real work.

The firms that will win are not simply those that have the best AI tools. They are those with the clearest strategy, the strongest data foundations, the most engaged people, and the most thoughtful governance.

This is not a comfortable reality. It is easier to blame the tool, or the market, or the difficulty of change. It is harder to ask whether we actually know our own business well enough. Do we have the leadership bandwidth to drive change? Are we brave enough to question what has always worked before? Are we willing to admit that we might need to work entirely differently?

But this is also liberating. It means you are not passive. You are not waiting for the perfect algorithm or the next ChatGPT release to make the decision. You are not at the mercy of the market. You are in control of your own evolution. The outcome depends on you, not the technology.

YOUR STARTING POINT: SIX CONCRETE ACTIONS

You might now be reading this and thinking, 'I agree, but where do I actually start? I don't have unlimited time or resources. What is the minimum viable approach?' To get you started, here are six grounded, practical actions. Each maps back to the chapters in this book. Each is something you can do within the next week or two. Start with one, master it, and then move to the next. Treat these not as a linear sequence but as ingredients. Different organizations will mix them in different orders, and that is perfectly fine.

1. Have the Strategic Conversation (Chapter 3)

Gather the decision-makers in a room. This should not be a lunch where you discuss AI in passing, but a real conversation where you block out time to discuss the business holistically. What problems are you trying to solve with AI? Is it cost reduction? Quality improvement? Speed to market? Better client service? Competitive differentiation? Write down what success looks like in concrete, measurable terms. Not 'better efficiency' but 'reduce time-to-first-draft by 30%' or 'handle 50% of routine contract review without human involvement' or 'increase capacity without hiring'. Once you have clarity on the problem and the goal you have direction, and everything else flows from this.

2. Audit Your Data (Chapter 5)

Do you know what data you actually have? Is it structured (databases, matter data, pricing information) or unstructured (documents, emails, transcripts, messages)? Is it clean or scattered across systems? Is it accessible to the people who need it? Is it accurate? This is not a technology project, it is a discovery project. Spend meaningful time mapping out the landscape and talking to the people who work with the data every day. You will likely find that it is messier than you think, and that is entirely normal. That insight is valuable as it tells you where the real work ahead of you is.

3. Invest in Your People, Not Just the Tool (Chapter 6)

If you buy a tool but do not train your team, give them space to experiment, and align incentives around the outcomes you want, you will have an expensive tool that gathers dust. Assign someone (ideally two or three people) to deeply understand the technology and become internal champions. They should spend time with the tool, experiment, fail, and learn. Build a learning programme not a one-off training session, and make it clear that experimentation is valued and failures are expected. Show people why this matters to their work and their career, not just to the firm's bottom line. People follow conviction, not compliance.

4. Start Small, Learn Fast (Chapters 7 and 9)

Do not deploy across the entire firm at once. Pick one team, one practice area, one specific process. Maybe it is a contract review workflow or a due diligence process. Maybe it is memo drafting. Run a pilot that lasts four to six weeks. Measure what matters, like time saved, quality, *true and meaningful* adoption, and team sentiment. Learn what works and what does not. Iterate. Share learning openly, including failures. You will uncover real obstacles and opportunities that no consultant or vendor conversation will surface, and you will have a proof of concept that is real, rooted in your own business, and credible to the rest of the firm.

5. Build Governance that Enables, Not Prohibits (Chapters 8 and 9)

Establish clear guardrails for data protection, protection of client confidentiality, quality control, and secure handling of sensitive information. But do not strangle innovation with fear-based governance. The goal is responsible adoption, not preventing new ways of working. Ask what is actually at risk? What is the realistic worst case? What controls are needed to mitigate that risk? What would irresponsible use look like? Then establish only those controls and get out of the way. Trust the people you hired to exercise judgement. This is harder than just saying no. But 'no' on its own is never a strategy.

6. Connect with Others (Chapter 11)

You do not have to solve this alone. Join a community. Hire an experienced consultant. Go to a conference. Find peers at other firms who are navigating the same terrain. Create a virtual cohort if your geography does not support in-person gatherings. Share what you are learning. Share what did not work. Every conversation multiplies your knowledge by orders of magnitude. Every failure you learn from saves you from repeating it. Every success gives you templates to iterate on. This collective intelligence is one of your most valuable assets. And the most successful firms are usually also the most connected ones.

THE HORIZON

The pace of change in AI will not slow down. Within a year, the tools will be more capable; within three years, the landscape may be unrecognizable. Some of what you learn will be obsolete. Some of the investments you make will not pan out as expected, while some of the people who are excited today might lose interest. This is the nature of change.

Commit yourself to things that will not change: your judgement, your relationships, your integrity, your understanding of what your clients actually need. These are not commodities, and they cannot be automated. They are the soil from which all value grows.

Technology has always amplified human capability. A brilliant lawyer with a brilliant tool is extraordinary; a brilliant lawyer with a mediocre tool is still very good; a mediocre lawyer with a brilliant tool is still mediocre. AI is not a substitute for judgement, it is a lever. And like any lever, its power depends on what you are trying to move. The other weight is your responsibility.

There will be moments when you doubt this path. You will wonder if you are moving fast enough or if you are moving forward at all. You might see a competitor make a bold move and question whether your measured approach is right, or you might make a bold move yourself that does not immediately pay off. You might face a tool that does not work, a team that resists, a governance framework that feels cumbersome, or a strategic initiative that flops. These are not signs of failure but the texture of genuine change. Every successful adoption we have seen has been preceded by setbacks.

What matters is that you are thinking about it clearly. You are asking the right questions and grounding your decisions in strategy, data, and people, not just in the allure of new technology. The one thing you cannot afford to do is be passive, sit still, and do nothing. You should not be waiting for someone else to solve this problem, and you should not be hoping the technology will somehow fix things on its own. That is how we navigate this uncertainty: not with certainty but with clarity of purpose towards a better end and the willingness to adjust course when reality demands it.

A FINAL WORD

The legal profession has always been about expertise, judgement, trust, and advocacy. Those traits have not disappeared. Indeed, the need for them has expanded. Now, expertise includes understanding what AI can and cannot do, and why it matters. Judgment includes knowing when to rely on a tool and when to override it. Trust is built on transparency about how work is done, by whom, and for what purpose. Advice is amplified when you can move faster without losing quality.

Most firms will figure this out eventually. The question is whether you will figure it out intentionally or by accident, whether you will lead or follow, whether you will shape this moment or be shaped by it. The authors of this book believe that the best time to start is now, not in a year's time; not after waiting to see what happens, but today. The moment you close this book.

This book is not a roadmap with guaranteed outcomes. It is a framework for thinking, for asking the right questions, and for challenging assumptions. Use it to build conviction and confidence that you can navigate this moment, to connect with others who are grappling with the same questions and uncertainty.

Most of all, use it to remember you are not powerless, and nor are you a passenger. The future of your firm, your team, and your practice is not something that happens *to* you. It is something you create, deliberately and thoughtfully, through strategy, governance, processes, data, people, technology, and culture.

Go build something extraordinary.

Notes

Live, clickable links for the URLs that follow below are available at law-reinvented.com/notes.

CHAPTER I

1 Nick Hilborne, 'Legal tech investment hits record level in 2025', LegalFutures, 14 October 2025 (https://www.legalfutures.co.uk/latest-news/legal-tech-investment-hits-record-level-in-2025); and Joanna Glasner, 'Legal tech investment hits all-time high with Filevine funding', Crunchbase News, 23 September 2025 (https://news.crunchbase.com/venture/ai-legal-tech-investment-all-time-high-filevine).

2 Dylan Brown, 'The AI paradox: high adoption, low integration in law firms', LexisNexis, 7 September 2025 (https://www.lexisnexis.co.uk/blog/future-of-law/the-ai-paradox-high-adoption-low-integration-in-uk-law-firms); and Chris Frickland, 'Beyond the hype: why 95% of legal AI pilots fail (and your roadmap to success)', Axiom Law, September 2025 (https://www.axiomlaw.com/blog/legal-ai-pilots-fail-success-roadmap).

3 See https://skills.law/the-surveys.

4 See https://skills.law/legal-ai-dashboard.

5 David Jackson, 'Shoosmiths offers £1m bonus pot for 1 million AI prompts', Press Release, Shoosmiths, 2 April 2025 (https://www.shoosmiths.com/perspectives/news/shoosmiths-offers-1m-bonus-pot-for-1-million-ai-prompts).

6 See https://www.sra.org.uk/news/news/press/2025-press-releases/garfield-ai-authorised. See also Richard Tromans,

'AI-native law firm directory launches', Artificial Lawyer, 20 March 2026 (https://www.artificiallawyer.com/2026/03/30/ai-native-law-firm-directory-launches/).

7 Jamie Tso, 'The Jane Street of law: the rise of the Legal Quant – What happens when law meets systems thinking', 15 January 2026 (https://tsojamie.substack.com/p/the-jane-street-of-law-the-rise-of).

8 This is a reference to T. S. Eliot's 'The Hollow Men' and its closing lines: 'This is the way the world ends / Not with a bang but a whimper.' You can find 'The Hollow Men' in *T. S. Eliot's Poems, 1909–1925* (Faber & Faber Limited, 1925).

9 See https://www.sra.org.uk/news/news/press/2025-press-releases/garfield-ai-authorised.

10 Ben Rigby, 'SRA authorises new AI-powered law firm LawFairy – London-based firm uses "deterministic" AI platform to provide legal advice directly to clients', Global Legal Post, 24 February 2026 (https://www.globallegalpost.com/news/sra-authorises-new-ai-powered-law-firm-lawfairy-590898458).

11 Oz Benamram, 'From Uber to Lawber: how digital transformation may change the legal industry', law-ber.com, 19 April 2019.

CHAPTER 2

1 Megan Mulligan, 'How lawyers are using AI to draft better contracts faster', American Bar Association, 7 October 2025 (https://www.americanbar.org/groups/law_practice/resources/law-practice-today/2025/october-2025/lawyers-using-ai-to-draft-contracts/).

2 Tim Coles, 'Legal research using Generative AI', Thomson Reuters, 31 October 2025 (https://legalsolutions.thomsonreuters.co.uk/blog/2025/10/31/legal-research-using-generative-ai/).

3 Ashley Hallene and Jeffrey M. Allen, 'Using AI for predictive analytics in litigation', American Bar Association,

16 October 2024 (https://www.americanbar.org/groups/senior_lawyers/resources/voice-of-experience/2024-october/using-ai-for-predictive-analytics-in-litigation/).

4 Oliver Attinger, 'Legal vibe coding is taking off as lawyers turn side projects into working tools', Non-Billable, 30 January 2026 (https://www.nonbillable.co.uk/news/legal-vibe-coding-is-taking-off).

5 Cole Stryker and Jim Holdsworth, 'What is NLP (natural language processing)?', IBM (https://www.ibm.com/think/topics/natural-language-processing).

6 Choose Your Own Adventure® is a registered trademark of Chooseco LLC.

7 Ashish Vaswani, Noam Shazeer, Niki Parmar, Jakob Uszkoreit, Llion Jones, Aidan N. Gomez, Lukasz Kaiser, and Illia Polosukhin, 'Attention is all you need', Preprint, arXiv 1706.03762 (submitted 12 June 2017; revised 2 August 2023).

8 Emerging Technology from the arXiv, 'King – Man + Woman = Queen: the marvelous mathematics of computational linguistics', Technology Review, 17 September 2014 (https://www.technologyreview.com/2015/09/17/166211/king-man-woman-queen-the-marvelous-mathematics-of-computational-linguistics).

9 Visual Storytelling Team and Madhumita Murgia, 'Generative AI exists because of the transformer', *Financial Times*, 12 September 2023 (https://ig.ft.com/generative-ai).

10 GPT stands for generative pre-trained transformer.

11 BERT stands for bidirectional encoder representations from transformers.

12 Sam Altman (@sama) on X, 5 December 2022 (https://x.com/gdb/status/1599683104142430208).

13 Dan Milmo and agency, 'ChatGPT reaches 100 million users two months after launch', *The Guardian*, 2 February 2023 (https://www.theguardian.com/technology/2023/feb/02/chatgpt-100-million-users-open-ai-fastest-growing-app).

14 Dan Milmo, 'Two US lawyers fined for submitting fake court citations from ChatGPT', *The Guardian*, 23 June 2023 (https://www.theguardian.com/technology/2023/jun/23/two-us-lawyers-fined-submitting-fake-court-citations-chatgpt).

15 Catherine Bamford, 'I tried to draft a lease with GenAI so I could test my own assumptions', LinkedIn, 3 March 2026 (https://www.linkedin.com/pulse/i-tried-draft-lease-genai-so-could-test-my-own-catherine-bamford-dknke).

CHAPTER 3

1 Richard Susskind, 'Moses to the modern law firm', *Forbes*, 21 March 2014 (https://www.forbes.com/sites/davidparnell/2014/03/21/richard-susskind-moses-to-the-modern-law-firm).

2 William Stanley Jevons, *The Coal Question: An Inquiry Concerning the Progress of the Nation, and the Probable Exhaustion of our Coal-mines*, ed. A. W. Flux, 3rd edn (Augustus M. Kelley, New York, 1905).

CHAPTER 4

1 Jamie Tso, 'The Jane Street of law: the rise of the Legal Quant – What happens when law meets systems thinking', 15 January 2026 (https://tsojamie.substack.com/p/the-jane-street-of-law-the-rise-of).

2 See Adam Curphey's *The Legal Team of the Future: Law+ Skills* (London Publishing Partnership, 2022) for in-depth discussions of lawyers having the skills required in an I-shaped, T-shaped, O-shaped, delta-shaped, or +-shaped skills model (https://londonpublishingpartnership.co.uk/books/the-legal-team-of-the-future-law-skills/).

3 Dan Milmo, 'Leading law firm cuts London back-office staff as it embraces AI', *The Guardian*, 21 November 2025 (https://www.theguardian.com/technology/2025/nov/21/

increased-ai-use-law-firm-clifford-chance-cuts-london-jobs-10-per-cent).

CHAPTER 5

1 L. Wachowski and L. Wachowski, *The Matrix* (Warner Bros, 1999).
2 Taylor Brownlow, 'Dashboards are dead', Medium.com, 9 April 2020; Taylor Brownlow, 'Dashboards are dead: 3 years later', Medium.com, 12 April 2023.
3 Nick Hilborne, 'Legal tech investment hits record level in 2025', LegalFutures, 14 October 2025 (https://www.legalfutures.co.uk/latest-news/legal-tech-investment-hits-record-level-in-2025).

CHAPTER 6

1 Nick Lichtenberg, 'Meet David Joyner, the professor who cloned himself with an AI avatar named "DAI-vid", as part of an experiment to "democratize" online learning', *Fortune*, 15 October 2025 (https://fortune.com/2025/10/15/the-ai-upskilling-tsunami-edx-open-course-agarwal-mit-joyner-georgia-tech).
2 B. M. Bloom, *Learning for Mastery*, pp. 1–12 (Center for the Study of Evaluation of Instructional Programs, 1968).
3 Alex Alridge, 'Profession prepares for big changes in training of lawyers', Legal Cheek, 31 May 2019 (https://www.legalcheek.com/2019/05/profession-prepares-for-big-changes-in-training-of-lawyers); Matthew J. Homewood, 'Law schools, the SQE and technology', LegalFutures, 26 February 2020 (https://www.legalfutures.co.uk/blog/law-schools-the-sqe-and-technology).
4 Legal IT Insider, 'Joe Cohen joins Harvey as legal innovation partner', 18 February 2026 (https://legaltechnology.com/2026/02/18/joe-cohen-joins-harvey-as-legal-innovation-partner); Artificial Lawyer, 'Harvey hires Tara Waters',

3 March 2026 (https://www.artificiallawyer.com/2026/03/03/harvey-hires-tara-waters).

5 At the time of writing, LinkedIn cited 978 legal innovation jobs in the United Kingdom.

6 Lawrence Akka KC, chair of the Bar Council of England and Wales's IT Panel, has said that witness statements should be written in the witness's own words and that people 'should not be able to generate, alter, embellish or rephrase their statements using AI' (Bar Council Press Release, 21 April 2026 (https://www.barcouncil.org.uk/resource/professional-standards-ai.html)).

7 Legal IT Insider, 'Clio completes $1bn acquisition of vLex + raises $500m Series G at $5bn valuation', 10 November 2025 (https://legaltechnology.com/2025/11/10/clio-completes-1bn-acquisition-of-vlex-raises-500m-series-g-at-5bn-valuation).

8 Legal Cheek, 'Ropes & Gray encourages junior lawyers to spend 20% of billable time on AI', 19 November 2025 (https://www.legalcheek.com/2025/11/ropes-gray-encourages-juniors-to-spend-20-of-billable-hours-on-ai).

CHAPTER 7

1 See https://www.legaltechnologyhub.com.

2 See https://skills.law/the-surveys.

3 For further detail on process mapping see Ryan Tronier, 'What is process mapping? Steps, types, examples & template', Asana, 11 February 2026 (https://asana.com/resources/process-mapping); Adam Curphey, *The Legal Team of the Future: Law+ Skills* (London Publishing Partnership, 2022) (https://londonpublishingpartnership.co.uk/books/the-legal-team-of-the-future-law-skills/).

4 For one such framework see Jitendra Kumar, 'The AI prioritization framework: how to know where to invest first', Medium, 24 January 2026 (https://medium.com/@contact.jitendra07/the-ai-prioritization-framework-how-to-know-where-to-invest-first-a7544220cd4b).

5 See chapter 2 on Model Context Protocol; chapter 5 on MCP and the opening of legal data; and chapter 9 on lawyer-built solutions and shadow AI.
6 Simon Lock, '40% of UK top 50 firms lack top UK cybersecurity certification, research shows', Law.com, 19 February 2021 (https://www.law.com/international-edition/2021/02/19/40-of-uk-top-50-firms-lack-top-uk-cybersecurity-certification-research-shows).

CHAPTER 8

1 See, for example, the Aderant report from 2018 titled 'Challenging the status quo in law firms: a legal business report by Aderant' (https://www.aderant.com/wp-content/uploads/2018/02/Status-Quo-Gen-LBR-NA-012918.pdf) or the LexisNexis discussion paper 'The Bellwether Report 2018. A dangerous allegiance to the status quo?' (https://www.lexisnexis.co.uk/bellwether/assets/pdfs/LN_Bellwether_Roundtable_14.pdf).
2 *United States v. Heppner*, No. 25-cr-00503 (SDNY, February 2026).
3 *Warner v. Gilbarco, Inc.*, No. 2:2024cv12333, Document 94 (ED Michigan 2026).
4 Cleary Gottlieb, 'Courts grapple with privilege implications of AI', Alert Memorandum, 27 February 2026 (https://www.clearygottlieb.com/-/media/files/alert-memos-2026/courts-grapple-with-privilege-implications-of-ai.pdf).
5 ABA Model Rules of Professional Conduct, Rule 1.1: Competence (https://www.americanbar.org/groups/professional_responsibility/publications/model_rules_of_professional_conduct/rule_1_1_competence).
6 SRA Code of Conduct for Solicitors, RELs, RFLs and RSLs, Paragraph 3: service and competence (https://www.sra.org.uk/solicitors/standards-regulations/code-conduct-solicitors).

7 See https://skills.law/the-surveys.

8 In relation to high-risk AI systems see 'Article 10: data and data governance' and 'Article 15: accuracy, robustness and cybersecurity' of the EU AI Act.

9 UNESCO, 'Ethics of artificial intelligence', UNESCO's Global AI Ethics and Governance Observatory (https://www.unesco.org/en/artificial-intelligence/recommendation-ethics).

10 Amanda Silberling, 'Your public ChatGPT queries are getting indexed by Google and other search engines', TechCrunch, 31 July 2025 (https://techcrunch.com/2025/07/31/your-public-chatgpt-queries-are-getting-indexed-by-google-and-other-search-engines).

11 *United States v. Heppner*, No. 25-cr-00503 (SDNY, February 2026).

12 *Warner v. Gilbarco, Inc.*, No. 2:2024cv12333, Document 94 (ED Michigan 2026).

13 *UK and R (on the application of Munir) v Secretary of State for the Home Department (AI hallucinations; supervision; Hamid)* [2026] UKUT 00081 (IAC).

14 See https://skills.law/the-surveys.

CHAPTER 9

1 Laura Cress, '"Vibe coding" named word of the year by Collins Dictionary', *BBC News*, 6 November 2025 (https://www.bbc.co.uk/news/articles/cpd2y053nleo).

2 Wix News Room, 'Wix further expands into vibe coding with acquisition of Base44, a hyper-growth startup that simplifies web and app creation with AI', Press Release, 18 June 2025 (https://www.wix.com/press-room/home/post/wix-further-expands-into-vibe-coding-with-acquisition-of-base44-a-hyper-growth-startup-that-simplif).

3 Andrej Karpathy (@karpathy) on X, 2 February 2025 (https://x.com/karpathy/status/1886192184808149383).

CHAPTER 10

1 Artificial Lawyer, 'Anthropic targets lawyers with Claude for Word', 11 April 2026 (https://www.artificiallawyer.com/2026/04/11/anthropic-targets-lawyers-with-claude-for-word/).
2 Orbital (referenced earlier) is now an AI-native law firm (https://www.artificiallawyer.com/2026/04/13/orbital-launches-its-own-real-estate-law-firm/).

CHAPTER 11

1 Colin Levy, 'Check out my all-new Legal Tech Resources Guide!', LinkedIn post, March 2026 (https://www.linkedin.com/posts/colinslevy_legal-tech-resource-guide-activity-7429185390680461312-3wJf/).
2 See https://cloc.org/.
3 See https://www.legalops.com/.
4 See https://www.iltanet.org/home.
5 See https://www.legalquants.com/.
6 See https://www.legaltechnologyhub.com/.
7 'Report and Recommendations of the New York State Bar Association Task Force on Artificial Intelligence', New York State Bar Association, 6 April 2024 (https://nysba.org/wp-content/uploads/2022/03/2024-April-Report-and-Recommendations-of-the-Task-Force-on-Artificial-Intelligence.pdf).
8 Law Society, 'Attitudes towards lawtech adoption', 28 June 2023 (https://www.lawsociety.org.uk/topics/research/read-our-new-report-on-attitudes-towards-lawtech-adoption); Law Society, 'AI and the law: the time to wait and see is over', 13 January 2026 (https://www.lawsociety.org.uk/topics/ai-and-lawtech/partner-content/ai-law-time-to-wait-and-see-is-over).
9 See https://lawtechuk.io.

About the Authors

Adam Curphey is Director of Innovation at a leading UK firm. Based in London he is also a visiting professor at BPP Law School and author of *The Legal Team of the Future: Law+ Skills.* Adam has worked at multiple law firms as both a practising lawyer and in his current role as a director of innovation, where he partners with lawyers, business teams, and clients to devise new ways of delivering legal services. He has been responsible for global AI strategy, amassed almost a decade of experience as a law and legal innovation lecturer, is a founding member of the in-house 'O Shaped' community, and has spoken on innovation and AI globally. Adam possesses a master's in law from University College, Oxford and a master's in education and technology from the UCL Institute of Education.

Oz Benamram is Chief AI and Knowledge Officer at a leading US firm, based in New York. A global leader in knowledge management and legal technology innovation, Oz has spent decades heading the knowledge and innovation functions at three leading law firms, and has advised law firm leaders, LegalTech companies, and investors on legal AI, knowledge, and innovation. He is the founder of SKILLS.law, a community of legal innovation professionals, and a frequent speaker, writer, and interviewer on the future of legal practice.

Rebecca Pasternak is Director, AI Integration & Enablement at a leading US law firm, based in New York. She is a technology and innovation leader with experience spanning legal practice, legal technology, venture-backed startups, and enterprise AI deployments. Rebecca has a proven track record designing and building enablement programmes that drive end-user adoption of new technology through core change management principles, and she possesses deep hands-on experience building with LLMs, with a genuine excitement for sharing what she has learned about how AI is reshaping ways of working, whether in hands-on training sessions or more broadly in public settings.

Index